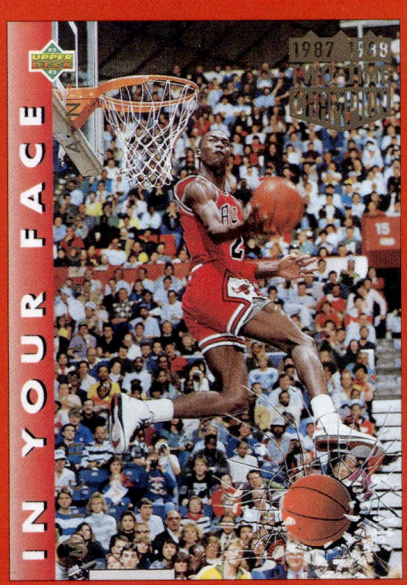

MICHAEL JORDAN COLLECTIBLES

Beckett

EVERYTHING YOU NEED TO KNOW ABOUT COLLECTING

BY THE STAFF OF BECKETT BASKETBALL CARD MONTHLY

MICHAEL JORDAN COLLECTIBLES

EVERYTHING
YOU NEED TO KNOW ABOUT
COLLECTING

MICHAEL JORDAN COLLECTIBLES

by the staff of *Beckett Basketball Monthly*.

Copyright©1998 by Dr. James Beckett

All rights reserved under International
and Pan-American Copyright Conventions.

Published by:
Beckett Publications
15850 Dallas Parkway
Dallas, TX 75248

ISBN: 1-887432-55-8

Beckett® is a registered trademark of Beckett Publications.

*Everything You Need To Know About Collecting
Michael Jordan Collectibles*

is not licensed, authorized or endorsed by any league,
player, or players assocation, nor is it authorized or
endorsed by Michael Jordan.

The prices on the following pages are based solely on the
knowledge and experience of the authors and dealers
across the country, as well as the expertise of
the editors of *Beckett Basketball Card Monthly*.
All figures are in U.S. dollars and are for entertainment
and informational purposes only.

First Edition: October 1998
Printed in Canada

Beckett Corporate Sales and Information
(972) 991-6657

BECKETT

Contents

How To Collect MJ Memorabilia	8
Autographs What You Need To Know	16
Basketball Cards	24
The Early Years (1954-85 to 1990-91)	26
The Wonder Years (1991-92 to 1994-95)	36
The Golden Years (1995-96 to Present)	52
Baseball Cards	72
How To Collect Jordan Autographs	82
Miscellaneous Price Guide	104
Supercollectors	128
Market Analysis	144

HOW TO COLLECT MJ MEMORABILIA

How To Collect MJ Memorabilia

By Randy Cummings

If there's a key to collecting Michael Jordan memorabilia, you need look no further than The Man himself. Like MJ in a critical game, with time ticking away and the defense swarming and his Chicago Bulls in need of a basket, you've got to be in control.

Control in the sense of knowing what you want — anything with Jordan's image on it, right? — how you want to go about getting it, and what you're going to do with it once you get it.

Michael's global popularity means he's easily the most collected athlete of our era. His place in the world of sports and sports memorabilia were established long ago, giving both casual fans and serious collectors a reason and a means of acquiring Michael Jordan . . . stuff.

If you want it, it's out there.

And if it's got Jordan's picture or a likeness of his bald dome or his replica signature or his Chicago Bulls jersey No. 23 or the soaring Air Jordan corporate logo on it, consider it an MJ collectible. And hang on to it, because chances are, you'll never want to get rid of it anyway.

"I would say that 90 percent of the people who collect Jordan never have

MICHAEL JORDAN COLLECTIBLES **9**

HOW TO COLLECT MJ MEMORABILIA

HOW TO COLLECT MJ MEMORABILIA

any intention of selling (their collection)," says Tim Jostes, a Chicago-area Jordan memorabilia dealer who owns Magoo's Collectibles in nearby Lansing, Ill. "Most of the people I sell to buy his stuff because they want a part of history.

"Memorabilia is exactly what it says: memories. It's something to remember him by."

And above all, Jostes adds, keep it fun.

But where to begin? Any card store in the world, of course, will be well-stocked in Jordan sports cards. Look closer and chances are you can have your pick of framed photos, posters, figurines and any number of other Jordan items to purchase. Go to a card show and the available MJ stock might expand to jerseys, shoes, cereal boxes, ticket stubs, buttons, books, pocket schedules and any other imaginable item that can hold his image.

Most toy stores and retail outlets also will have Jordan somewhere on their shelves. And during the season, Jordan will appear on countless magazine covers, another popular keepsake.

For those who enjoy shopping from home, today's computer technology provides virtual no-limits access via the Internet to Jordan memorabilia and Jordan memorabilia collectors worldwide.

Just remember, always stay in control. If there is a golden rule in sports memorabilia collecting, it's that you should collect only the items you enjoy and can afford. This certainly applies to Jordan collectibles, which can range in value from the five-figure prices on his game-worn jerseys and the thousands commanded for his highly scarce Star Company cards of the early 1980s, down to today's over-produced issues that can easily be pulled from a pack.

"It should be fun to collect," Jostes notes. "This should be something you do because you want to do it. Buy what you can afford. Collect what you like. After all, you're going to be the one looking at it."

Two other things to consider when collecting Michael Jordan: 1) It's unlikely you'll ever acquire every Jordan card, magazine cover or whatever is out there. So don't even try. And, 2) Because of the volume of MJ collectibles, don't ever expect to complete your search. It's a journey with no end.

So why not get started? And don't forget to have fun.

HOW TO COLLECT MJ MEMORABILIA

Four-step Plan

COLLECTING SPORTS PUBLICATIONS CAN BE AS EASY AS ONE, TWO, THREE . . . AND FOUR.

Sports publications have taken on a renaissance. Collectors are discovering that publications from ballparks and stores have more to offer than a baseball card without gum. Besides, collecting them is fun and relatively inexpensive.

However, several vital steps must be taken to develop an enjoyable and long-lasting publication collection.

Often, collectors head into so many directions that they get lost somewhere along the way and wish they had created a different, less-complicated game plan.

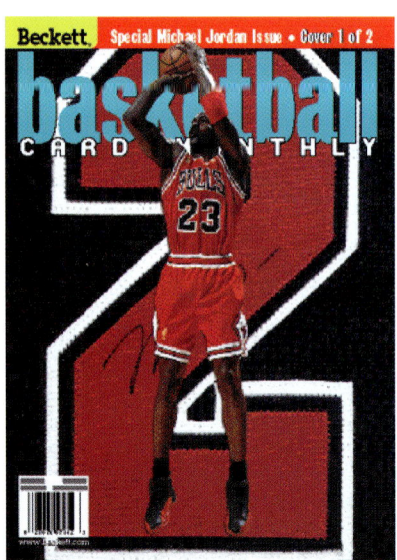

Generating your own publications collection can be done with ease by following these four steps:

1. HAVE A PLAN

So why do you want to collect publications? Do you have a favorite player, team and sport? Do you have a favorite magazine? Do you want to collect a favorite event (Jordan in the NBA Finals, for example)?

What ever it is, you need to have a plan. The plan dictates a sequence of steps in building your collection. Plans also make it easier to work with fellow collectors and dealers because they can assist you with your needs.

A plan can be as simple as collecting NBA Finals programs or the complete run of *Beckett Basketball Card Monthly*.

Whatever the focus or theme is, write it down. Part of a quality plan is to put it to paper. Putting the plan to paper helps you pinpoint your goals and it adds as a written checklist for what you have in your collection and what you still need. I collect Time and Sports Illustrated. However, I narrowed the focus of my plan to Mint Time and Sport Illustrated magazines.

The plan can consist of at least two parts. The first part is determining what you need and the second part deals with getting the magazines.

2. IMPLEMENT A PLAN OF ACTION/ CREATE WANT LISTS AND INVENTORY LISTS

Want lists and inventory lists serve as road maps toward completing your collection.

So many collectors rely on their memory and sometimes buy the same magazine twice or pass up a publication that they may never see again. Guides are helpful in compiling want lists because they provide information related to who is on the cover, content, values, etc.

However, most guides do not compile lists of players and therefore you need to find other collectors who may have lists. One exception is the *Collectors Guide to Sports Illustrated and Sports Publications* that has an alpha player index on SI, Sport, *Beckett*, etc. that is helpful.

Some of the best lists in the world are compiled by advanced player or team collectors. For example, Nolan News has one of the most comprehensive lists of Nolan Ryan magazines ever produced.

Also, a Mets collectors club has

HOW TO COLLECT MJ MEMORABILIA

MICHAEL JORDAN COLLECTIBLES **13**

HOW TO COLLECT MJ MEMORABILIA

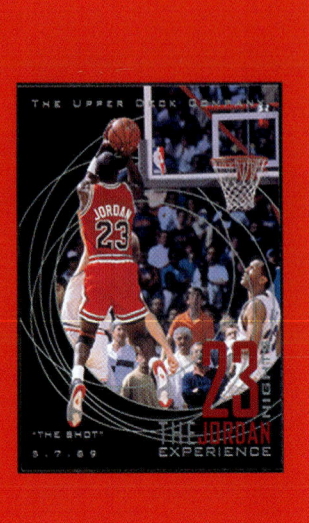
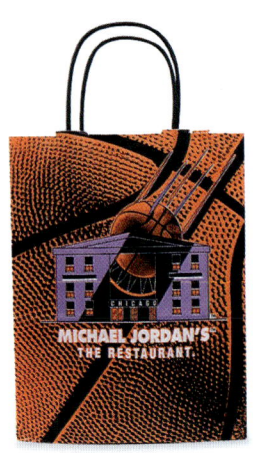

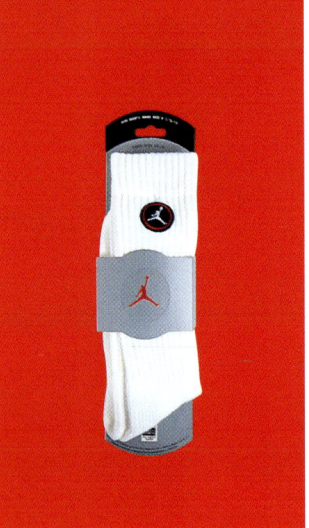
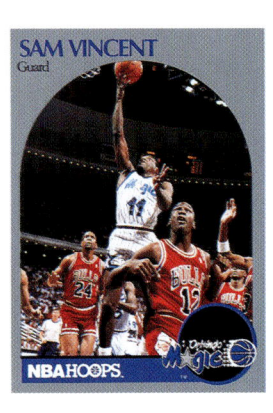

HOW TO COLLECT MJ MEMORABILIA

compiled a quality list of Mets publications.

If you can't find a list that matches your theme or focus, create one. The first step is to catalog what you have in your collection. Secondly, compile a list of magazines that you know exist and need for your collection.

Major dealers create sales lists that you can find both new items as well as items for your collection. Tedious labor is involved, but you will enjoy the process and other collectors will appreciate your work.

Catalog your publications list in a database or a spreadsheet and send it to fellow collectors and dealers in and out of town. Not only can they help you find the publications you need, but if they also can provide additional information to your list or comments on better methods of chronicling them.

3. COLLECT THE BEST

Always buy quality. If you're picking up a publication from the newsstand, get Mint copies only.

For example, a *Beckett* magazine used as a Price Guide has little value to a Beckett collector. However, a Mint copy still is worth its cover value (and maybe more) to a fellow collector.

If it's a publication you're likely to keep in your collection for the long run, grab the best copy you can find.

Some collectors believe the fallacy that all grades are the same. The price gaps between the grades is not as great as baseball cards, but you can bet in the future the gap between a Mint 1983 Jordan ($190-$200-plus range) is going to increase from an EX-MT ($100) or VG-EX ($30) condition Sports Illustrated. This may not apply for magazines that you are buying for

articles, pictures or ads (EX-MT is satisfactory here). This also does not apply for rare material where the best you may ever see is an EX-MT grade magazine.

Buying "filler" issues saves some heartache. For example, if you're a Tiger Woods collector and you stumble across the December 1996 Sports Illustrated for Kids issue that features Woods' first card, buy it regardless of the condition. It can serve as a "filler" until you can find a Mint copy. It's never safe to assume that you'll find a Mint copy of the magazine you're hunting.

4. GO SHOPPING

I am a dealer who would love to sell you magazines. However, I recommend that you run ads in a local newspaper if you're serious about collecting publications.

Also, hit the garage sales, visit the flea market and go through your local yellow pages. Many new and used magazine shops exist that can be a gold mine for publication collectors. Create business cards and leave them with those used magazine stores. The stores often will notify you if they receive something you're interested in. All of these leads may lead to nowhere or they could lead to a treasure find.

Phil Regli, a leading expert on sports publications, can be contacted through his Internet site: Asportmall.com.

AUTOGRAPHS WHAT YOU NEED TO KNOW

AUTOGRAPHS

What you need to know

Want Michael's autograph? Then be prepared to pay . . . and wait.

Collectors who long for Jordan's signature better have deep pockets and plenty of patience. Getting the real deal when it comes to Jordan ceased being a matter luck a long time ago. Landing a legit autograph from the world's most famous basketball player — perhaps the most recognized athlete on earth — is no longer a matter of catching him after a game, at the Bulls' hotel or coming off the 18th hole at some swank country club.

That's not how the game is played when it comes to Michael Jordan, who travels in secrecy and comes complete with a staff of bodyguards when he dares to make an appearance in public. He's untouchable before and after games, enters and exits hotels during the season like a rock star being protected from screaming fans, and gets so much fan mail that it's impossible for him to read it, much less respond to it. So he doesn't.

BY RANDY CUMMINGS

Today, there are virtually two means of getting MJ's autograph. One way involves chance while the second method boasts logic. For the record, most memorabilia experts, albeit somewhat grudgingly, support the latter.

"I hate to say it, but Upper Deck Authenticated is probably the best way to get the real thing," says one of those experts, Chicago-based memorabilia man Tim Jostes.

UDA, the sports memorabilia branch of the Upper Deck sports card manufacturer, owns a contract with the Bulls' superstar that essentially gives them ownership of Jordan's autograph. Oh, you can always buy a Jordan-signed item off a show table or shop shelf — that's the first way to land his autograph — but collectors are taking a

AUTOGRAPHS WHAT YOU NEED TO KNOW

good risk that the piece has been forged.

Therefore, the smart collector takes the safe route and coughs up the money to purchase a Jordan-signed photo, basketball, jersey, or whatever, directly from UDA. With the bill of sale comes the comfort of knowing the autograph was, in fact, written by Michael himself. Their contract with Michael provides all the backbone UDA needs for its Certificates of Authenticity.

There's a catch, however. The demand for UDA items containing authentic Jordan autographs became so great that the company had to stop tak-

CHICAGO BULL
1984 – 1993

The best there ever was. The best there ev

**DEDICATED
NOVEMBER 1, 1994**

AUTOGRAPHS WHAT YOU NEED TO KNOW

AUTOGRAPHS WHAT YOU NEED TO KNOW

ing orders, at least momentarily, early in 1998. Jordan couldn't sign fast enough to keep up, which has led to a waiting list for back orders that now extends to nearly a full year.

Collectors who can't wait that long or don't want to order through UDA, most autographs experts agree, are taking a serious chance in an unfortunate era of mass forgeries meant at collecting a quick buck. It may look like Michael's handwriting, but the odds are stacked against it being the real deal.

"Common sense needs to be used tremendously," Jostes says. "You've got to deal with a person you know and trust. You don't buy Michael Jordan memorabilia at a flea market. And if a price is too good to be true, it probably isn't true."

There's one other advantage to seeking Jordan's autograph through UDA: variety. Because of its access to His Airness, UDA can offer Jordan's signature on such unique items as an official major league baseball, a Chicago White Sox batting helmet or a No. 45 Bulls jersey.

MICHAEL JORDAN COLLECTIBLES 23

Basketball Cards Introduction

Basketball Card Introduction

There was a time, believe it or not, when collectors couldn't have cared less about basketball cards. Even Michael Jordan cards. In the mid-1980s, Jordan's two key issues — his 1984-85 Star Extended Rookie Card and his mainstream 1986-87 Fleer RC — could have been purchased in a package deal for around 10 bucks.

My, how things have changed.

Today, a deal for those two Jordan issues, assuming the cards are in top condition, will set a collector back the equivalent of a down payment on a house in the suburbs. They stand easily as the most cherished, not to mention expensive, cards of their time.

In fact, the '84-85 Star Jordan XRC stands in a class of its own: No other mainstream card of an active or recently retired athlete in any sport comes near matching its value of about $3,000. And of all of Michael's cards, none has equaled his '86-87 Fleer RC in popularity or notoriety. Featuring a photo that captures Jordan in midflight on the way to one of his classic thundering jams, its current value of about $1,000 dwarfs all others in that famous 132-card set.

And it's not just the old cards. Several of Jordan's later releases have skyrocketed in value. The 1997-98 Metal Universe Precious Metal Gems Green #23 lists at $8,500. And even that pales in comparison to the '97-98 Upper Deck Game Jersey Autograph #GJ13s, listed at a remarkable $10,000.

So why have Jordan's cards — just about every one of the 1,500 released before the 1998-99 season — become so highly regarded? Even before Michael's foray into baseball and his storybook return to the hardcourt, the demand for his cards was so strong that collectors were willing to shell out hundreds, even thousands, of dollars for the more desirable Jordan issues.

The reason? Supply and demand. In the minds of most collectors, and most basketball fans in general, MJ is the best player of his generation. Period.

Jordan's enormous popularity continues to have a direct impact on his collectibles. For example, another highly touted rookie has his RC in the same 1986-87 Fleer set as Jordan. Although nobody in their right mind would say the retired Clyde Drexler is every bit the player Jordan is, The Glide certainly had, by anyone else's standards, a spectacular NBA career. But Clyde's card is valued at a fraction of Michael's card, which is certainly not an indication that Jordan is 10 times the player that Drexler was. In truth, the huge difference in values of the two cards relates directly to Jordan's status as a worldwide hero.

But not every good-looking, highly regarded Jordan card will cost you an arm and a leg. Several sharp cards are valued at less than $10, including the 1996-97 Stadium Club Shining Moments #SM2 ($5), with a shot of a one-handed tomahawk jam, and the '97-98 Collector's Choice Crash The Game Redemption #R30 ($8), featuring a photo of a fadeaway jumper.

Jordan's impact on card collectors goes even further than value. In the mid-'80s, basketball cards were basically shunned by hobbyists, most of whom zealously pursued baseball cards. But now, looking back on Jordan's success and the high value of his rookie cards, any hoops prospect with the slightest amount of hype coming out of college (or high school) has such a huge following in the hobby that his cards leave a scorch on every collector's want list.

Examples are plentiful — Shaquille O'Neal, Grant Hill, Allen Iverson, Kevin Garnett. . . . These guys owe much of their early hobby success to Jordan. But in the end, hobbyists across the world agree: There's only one MJ.

1984-1991 THE EARLY YEARS

Fueled by Michael Jordan's RC, '86-87 Fleer overcame initial disinterest 12 years ago to become the basketball hobby's...

LANDMARK SET

In terms of significance to the hobby of basketball card collecting, perhaps the most important set ever to come flying off a printing press is the 1986-87 Fleer issue.

It's become a landmark set whose place in hobby history is forever secure. It's hard to pinpoint another single basketball set whose cards are so highly regarded by today's collectors.

Fleer's '86-87 issue, a 132-card set whose overall design pales by today's glittery standards, contains possibly the greatest selection of Rookie Cards ever featured in one set. Mint and well-centered singles are elusive enough to keep investment-oriented collectors interested, yet in general the cards are available for hobbyists of all ages to pursue.

"Without a doubt, it's the best basketball set ever issued," says Mark Murphy, one of the hobby's leading dealers in unopened packs and boxes (and a regular contributor to *Beckett Basketball Monthly*).

Not only is the set a significant one for collectors, but also for the company that produced it. The set marked Fleer's return to the basketball market after a 25-year absence and set the stage for Fleer to become a big-time player in the hobby.

No wonder Fleer honored the classic issue with a commemorative insert set, Decade of Excellence, that appeared in its '96-97 Fleer basketball release "[The '86-87 set] is the keystone to our

BY GRANT SANDGROUND

entire basketball product line," says Ted Taylor, Fleer's hobby division vice president. "That set helped propel us from a one-sport company into further avenues of expansion."

Many basketball collectors look upon the '86-87 Fleer set in the same light that baseball card collectors view the 1952 Topps set. Each set has become the creme de la creme of its respective sport. A brand loyalty exists among the many thousands of baseball card collectors who grew up collecting Topps cards. And slowly, that same sort of pattern is forming in basketball — in part because of Fleer's 12-year run in the hobby. And the 1986-87 Fleer set is where it all began.

"There's a basketball legacy here at Fleer," Taylor agrees.

THE EARLY YEARS 1984-1991

A SHOT AT HOOPS

As difficult as it may be for some younger hobbyists to comprehend, 12 years ago Fleer's only major sports card product was baseball. Then the NBA came calling.

"The [Fleer] president at that time was Donald Peck," Taylor says. "He was looking to expand properties. We had been issuing a [team-focused] football set in previous years, but it wasn't very good. When the NBA offered Fleer a deal, Peck jumped on the opportunity. We signed a three-year agreement with the NBA and were going to see what happened from there. We created an excellent foundation for a relationship with the NBA when we signed that deal."

But don't be fooled. Fleer's first basketball product since its first and only other shot with its 1961-62 set wasn't an instant hit. In fact, it fared poorly. It's hard to imagine, but 10 years ago the set was considered somewhat of a flop.

"It was a very rocky first year," Taylor says. "We didn't sell a lot of product. There was a low production run to begin with and we took a lot of returns that year."

Among those few collectors who showed an interest in the cards, sets routinely retailed for between $8 and $15. Dealers regularly offered entire cases for as little as $99 each (about $5 per box). Packs sold for about 50 cents each.

And inside those packs, one of the hottest cards that could be pulled featured . . . Spud Webb. Upon the set's release, Webb's card (#120) actually was more popular than Michael Jordan's issue (#57). The diminutive Webb, as a rookie in 1985-86, had won the '86 Slam Dunk event and his Fleer card pictures one of his contest-winning jams.

This isn't to say collectors weren't interested in Michael's card. The Jordan RC was a decent seller — at about a dollar!

At the time of its release, '86-87 Fleer represented the first mainstream basketball issue from a major manufacturer in four years. During that span, basketball collectors saw stars in their eyes; the relatively small Star Company satisfied their hunger for cards by issuing attractive team sets through a network of hobby dealers. Star Company cards were licensed by the NBA and even today are considered legitimate mainstream issues.

Yet, due to their small print runs, quirky distribution and rampant counterfeiting scares in today's market, Star Company cards got overlooked by many collectors. This hobby mind-set has greatly benefited Fleer's premier release as hobbyists now consider many players' first Fleer cards as their true Rookie Cards.

SEEING STARS

The timing was perfect for the '86-87 Fleer set. Its lineup of RCs for future Hall of Famers remains unparalleled. It's nearly impossible to pick another set, in any sport, that can match Fleer's roster of RC heavyweights such as Jordan, Charles Barkley (#7), Clyde Drexler (#26), Joe Dumars (#27), Patrick Ewing (#32), Karl Malone (#68), Hakeem Olajuwon (#82), Isiah Thomas (#109) and Dominique Wilkins (#121).

MICHAEL JORDAN
BULLS • GUARD-FORWARD

1984-1991 THE EARLY YEARS

Despite the phenomenal selection of superstars in the '86-87 Fleer set, there are some significant no-shows.

The most obvious is Utah's legendary playmaker John Stockton. He was featured on a number of Star Company cards preceding this set, yet he didn't make his Fleer debut until 1988-89 (#115). Seattle forward Detlef Schrempf (then a member of the Dallas Mavericks) and NBA ironman A.C. Green of the Dallas Mavericks also are notable exclusions.

A.C. Green's absence is interesting because he appears in the background of several other players' cards; he's particularly visible on George Gervin's #36 and Bill Hanzlik's #43. Green's unofficial appearances in the set can be traced to the fact that nearly every photo used for the set was taken in Los Angeles at either a Lakers or Clippers home game.

If there is a major drawback to the set, it's the frequency with which cards are found off-center. Poor centering was quite common for most issues produced in the mid-1980s. And the '86-87 Fleer design, with its framed inner border and bright red corners, was an easy target for potential printing and handling problems.

"There's no shortage of 1986-87 Fleer cards on the market today," says basketball card expert and national dealer Steve Taft, owner of Steve Taft Enterprises. "There is just a shortage of truly Mint and centered 1986-87 Fleer cards."

Dealers and collectors often focus on the quality of centering on cards, with numbers referring to the percentage that each border shares to the edge of the card. A 50/50 card is perfectly centered while a 90/10 card has one border that is drastically wider than the other. Because most '86-87 Fleer cards are found off-center, the monthly BKM Price Guide lists values for Near Mint-Mint condition, cards that are centered 55/45 or better.

Collectors lucky enough to find '86-87 Fleer cards that exceed these standards generally can expect a sale price of 100 to 150 percent of book value — and sometimes as high as 200 percent of book value for cards that are particularly tough to find well centered.

"I've been opening boxes since they were $15 a piece [in the mid-'80s] and I've seen some with poorly centered cards all the way through," Taft says. "Sometimes you're lucky to get 20 to

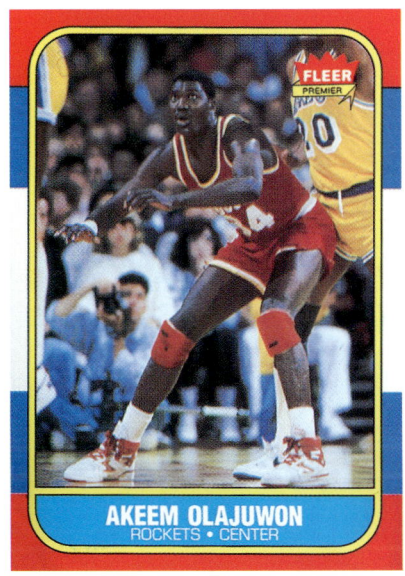
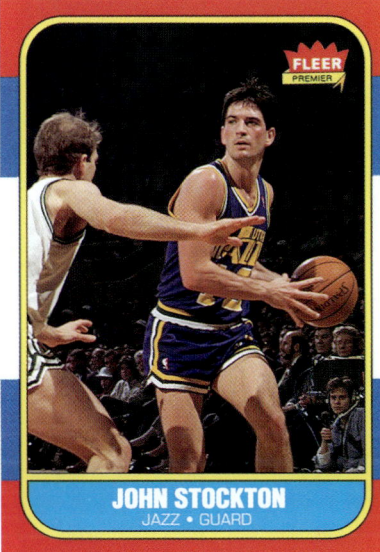

THE EARLY YEARS 1984-1991

THE LOOK

THE ORIGINAL DESIGNER OF THE '86-87 FLEER SET DISCUSSES THE CREATION OF THE HOBBY'S PIVOTAL ISSUE

Joe Nixon was the creative designer behind the 1986-87 Fleer issue. Currently senior manager of design and technology, Nixon reflected on the landmark issue with former *Beckett Basketball Monthly* associate editor Randy Cummings in the fall of 1996.

BKM: What was your position and role with Fleer back in 1986?

Nixon: At that time I was art director, handling the production from a prepress standpoint.

BKM: When Fleer made the decision to produce the '86-87 basketball set, what were some of the directives made to you as far as the objectives Fleer had with this set?

Nixon: At the time, Fleer was a pretty small group of people. There wasn't an in-depth set of instructions when we developed a new product. We looked at the competition, looked at new designs — I was doing the designing at that time — and then we came up with what we thought was the best presentation.

At the time, we were getting away from the gray backs and we went right to white paper on both sides. And at least with basketball, we hadn't gotten into full color on both sides — but we were looking at it. I probably did a dozen different designs. We mulled them over and picked the one that we finally used.

BKM: What do you recall about the photo selection, the quality of photos at that time, that was available to you?

Nixon: It doesn't match today's quality, of course. And today, the NBA provides all the photography. At the time, I think we still were using freelance photographers. They didn't have all the lighting that's available today, so the quality of the photographs wasn't what it is today. And the shots were from different angles, farther back. You just didn't get the variety or quality that you get today.

BKM: Do you recall some of the discussions about creating the sticker set?

Nixon: I know there were still some questions about how acceptable stickers would be as a collectible and they just didn't want to leave that stone unturned. I think they wanted to produce a sticker to see just how successful it might be.

BKM: When you look back at that set and consider the place in the history of the basketball hobby that it's created for itself, what are your feelings?

Nixon: (laughing) Well, we all owe a lot to Michael Jordan, I guess. I'm shocked at some of the quotes for prices for boxes and cases and those cards that have remained untouched. It's just amazing. It makes me regret I never put any aside for myself.

BKM: As a creative person, how do you look back on the design of the set?

Nixon: I still like that design, personally, when I compare it to some of the other early card designs that we did at Fleer. I think it's one that's held up fairly well.

30 50/50 cards from a complete box of 432 cards. I once went through and pulled a 1,000-count lot and found only 17 50/50 centered cards. Truly centered cards get a definite premium over book values."

FRONT AND CENTER

Putting together a complete '86-87 Fleer set that is well centered is one of the hobby's toughest modern-day challenges.

"In general, the whole set is tough to find well centered," says veteran dealer Kris Keppfler. "I've been buying tons of sets lately and less than 10 percent of the cards I see are centered better than 60/40."

Throughout the years, certain cards in the set have gained reputations as being more difficult to locate without any centering problems. It's been Keppfler's experience that the cards of Wilkins, the checklist (#132) and Chris Mullin (#77) are among the toughest to find well centered.

Taft agrees that Mullin and Wilkins are high on the list, and is quick to add Ewing and Thomas.

Collectors who have tackled the challenge of putting a complete '86-87 Fleer set together are aware that even minor stars such as Derek Harper

1984-1991 THE EARLY YEARS

(#44), Eddie Johnson (#51), Bill Walton (#119) and Webb (#120) also pose centering problems. Some of the easier superstar cards to find reasonably well centered include Drexler, Malone and Olajuwon. Jordan's RC lies somewhere between.

Most collectors, fortunately, can pursue this set if they settle for relatively nice cards instead of demanding

Mint investment pieces.

"Sixty/forty or worse cards aren't tough to find," Taft says. "Basically, I think it's a set that's not too difficult to find at a reasonable price for a collector who's willing to settle for a lot of 70/30 to 60/40 cards."

Dealing with off-center cards is a palatable problem. Dealing with counterfeit cards is not.

No collector wants to be burned by coughing up big bucks for a fake card. And, unfortunately, the question looming on most collectors' minds these days when dealing with the '86-87 Fleer set is how to avoid purchasing a counterfeit card.

FAKED OUT

It's known that bogus cards of Barkley, Ewing, Jordan and Karl

Malone have been circulating in the hobby in recent years. Naturally, the Jordan card is the one most often duplicated.

"There are eight [counterfeit] versions of the Michael Jordan card," says Sally Grace, owner of Sally's Cards, a Chicago-area mail-order business, and one of the foremost authorities on counterfeit cards in the hobby. "There's no real one thing that can be singled out on each card. In general, the dot matrix, structure and weight of the cards all need to be looked at."

As the years have gone by, the fakes have gotten better and better. It takes years of experience to be able to ferret out the top-notch fakes.

The best advice for collectors is to buy from a dealer they know and trust. It's best to know that the dealer is experienced in '86-87 Fleer cards and will offer a money-back guarantee on the card if the buyer is not happy with it. A risk is being taken when purchasing a Fleer Jordan RC from a dealer who the collector may never see again.

On the other hand, there's a sense of security in buying from a local shop down the street that's been in business for the last five years or from a nationally known dealer who advertises regularly in the hobby trade publications.

One way hobbyists can be sure of getting legit '86-87 Fleer cards is pursuing unopened packs and boxes. It's a somewhat costly venture, but the thrill of opening a vintage pack that possibly contains some of the hobby's most famous issues is unmatched.

Busting open '86-87 Fleer packs is the equivalent of breaking open a fine bottle of wine; it'll cost you about the same amount of money, too. The allure

THE EARLY YEARS 1984-1991

STICKY SITUATION

OFTEN OVERLOOKED IN THE SHADOW OF THE SET'S MARQUEE CARDS, THE '86-87 FLEER STICKERS ARE A BARGAIN

If Michael Jordan's 1986-87 Fleer RC is valued at $1,000 or more, then it stands to question why his sticker in the set is only valued at around $100.

For such an early mainstream Jordan issue, his '86-87 Fleer Sticker (#8) can be labeled as

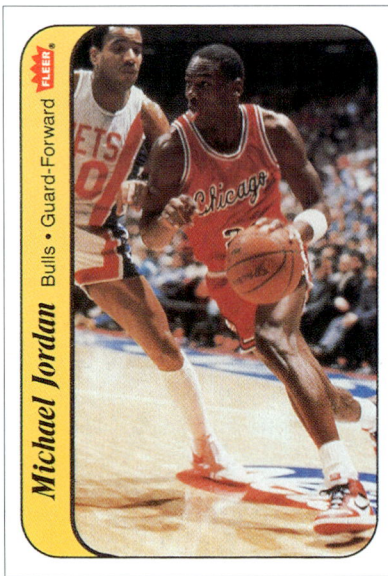

one of the better bargains in the hobby today.

The '86-87 Fleer Stickers are modestly valued. When collectors do the math on breaking down boxes, they get 36 stickers and 432 regular cards in each box. That breaks down to identical rates of 3.27 of each card or sticker per box.

"The demand isn't as strong for the stickers as it is for the regular cards," says basketball card specialist Steve Taft, owner of Steve Taft Enterprises. "Yet the production levels are so close that it's hard to explain why the stickers are valued so far below the regular cards."

Veteran dealer Kris Keppfler offers another theory: "The stickers sell as complete sets 50 percent of the time. Single stickers simply do not sell very well."

of finding a Jordan in a pack is a fantasy that nearly all basketball collectors share. Alas, only a handful can actually afford to live out this kind of dream.

"Packs generally retail around $200 each," says pack-specialist Murphy. "Complete boxes retail at around $6,000."

PACKING PUNCH

Here's what you get for your money: Each pack contains 12 cards, one sticker and a piece of gum, with boxes containing 36 packs. To assure that it's a vintage pack, Murphy offers the following advice:

• The corners of the pack should be folded like a birthday present would be wrapped. Bad packs have corners that are popped out and not neatly folded.

• The back of the pack has a roller-seal in the middle where the factory sealed the wax pack. An untampered seal should measure about 1-3/4 inches in diameter. It should be nice and clean, with no signs of wax being smeared. Any fingerprints are a red flag indication of possible tampering.

The best part about purchasing authentic '86-87 Fleer packs, of course, is that the buyer is assured of getting the real deal when the cards within are

revealed. Pulling out a piece of basketball card history is a joy that rarely can be duplicated today.

For sure, a lot has happened to the basketball card market since Fleer helped pump life back into it by taking the bold move of issuing a mainstream set in '86-87. Nowadays, in an age of inserts and interaction, collectors are offered glittery new basketball sets

seemingly every other week.

Still, the '86-87 Fleer set continues to stand as one of the elite glamour basketball issues. At a time when basketball cards were an afterthought to most collectors, Fleer took a chance. Thanks to a checklist second to none, its 1986-87 set will always rank as one of the hobby's most important issues ever printed.

Grant Sandground is the Price Guide editor for **Beckett Basketball Monthly.**

1984-1991 **THE EARLY YEARS**

PRICE GUIDE

Basketball Cards
1984-85 through 1990-91

Values were full retail selling prices at the time of publication, but it should be noted that lower prices can be found through extensive shopping. Cards from 1989-90 to present are valued in Mint, characterized by 60/40 or better centering, smooth edges, original color borders and gloss, and no print spots and color or focus imperfections. * denotes a multisport set.

THE EARLY YEARS 1984-1991

1984-85

Set	No.	Price
Star	101	3,000.00
Star	195	450.00
Star	288	450.00
Star Court Kings 5x7	26	275.00

1985-86

Set	No.	Price
Bulls Interlake	1	100.00
Bulls Team Issue	1	40.00
Prism/Jewel Stickers	7	400.00
Star	117	950.00
Star All-Rookie Team	2	300.00
Star Crunch'n'Munch All-Stars	4	350.00
Star Gatorade Slam Dunk	7	275.00
Star Last 11 ROY's	1	250.00
Star Lite All-Stars	4	250.00
Star Slam Dunk Supers 5x7	5	250.00
Star Team Supers 5x7	CB1	250.00

1986-87

Set	No.	Price
Fleer	57 RC	1000.00
Fleer Stickers	8	100.00
Star Best of the Best	9	125.00
Star Best of the New/Old	2	150.00
Star Court Kings	18	200.00
Star Michael Jordan	1	90.00
Star Michael Jordan	2	90.00
Star Michael Jordan	3	90.00
Star Michael Jordan	4	90.00
Star Michael Jordan	5	90.00
Star Michael Jordan	6	90.00
Star Michael Jordan	7	90.00
Star Michael Jordan	8	90.00
Star Michael Jordan	9	90.00
Star Michael Jordan	10	90.00

1987-88

Set	No.	Price
Bulls Entenmann's	23	100.00
Fleer	59	180.00
Fleer Stickers	2	40.00
Panini Spanish Stickers*	4	
Quaker Sports Illustrated Mini Posters	4	50.00

1988-89

Set	No.	Price
Bulls Entenmann's	23	60.00
Fleer	17	50.00
Fleer	120	20.00
Fleer Stickers	7	15.00
Fournier NBA Estrellas	22	8.00
Fournier NBA Estrellas Stickers	5	20.00
Panini Spanish Stickers	76	75.00
Panini Spanish Stickers	261	40.00
Panini Spanish Stickers	285	40.00

1984-1991 THE EARLY YEARS

1989-90

Set	No.	Price
Bulls Dairy Council	3	85.00
Bulls Equal	6	25.00
Fleer	21	10.00
Fleer Stickers	3	5.00
Hoops	21	1.50
Hoops	200	3.00
Hoops All-Star Panels	4	10.00
Magnetables	16	20.00
North Carolina Collegiate Collection	13	1.50
North Carolina Collegiate Collection	14	1.50
North Carolina Collegiate Collection	15	1.50
North Carolina Collegiate Collection	16	1.50
North Carolina Collegiate Collection	17	1.50
North Carolina Collegiate Collection	18	1.50
North Carolina Collegiate Collection	65	1.50
Panini Spanish Stickers	67	60.00
Panini Spanish Stickers	254	30.00
Sports Illustrated for Kids I *	16	35.00

1990-91

Set	No.	Price
Action Packed Promos *	3	250.00
Bulls Equal/Star	1	12.00
Fleer	26	2.00
Fleer All-Stars	5	6.00
Hoops	5	2.00
Hoops	65	2.00
Hoops	223A	1.50
Hoops	358	1.00
Hoops	382	1.00
Hoops	385	1.00
Hoops Action Photos	11	5.00
Hoops Action Photos	39	5.00
Hoops 100 Superstars	12	5.00
Hoops All-Star Panels	1	6.00
Hoops All-Star Panels	2	8.00
Hoops CollectABooks	4	5.00
Hoops Team Night Sheets	4	8.00
McDonald's Jordan/Joyner-Kersee *	1	2.00
McDonald's Jordan/Joyner-Kersee *	2	2.00
McDonald's Jordan/Joyner-Kersee *	3	2.00
McDonald's Jordan/Joyner-Kersee *	4	2.00
McDonald's Jordan/Joyner-Kersee *	5	2.00
McDonald's Jordan/Joyner-Kersee *	6	2.00
McDonald's Jordan/Joyner-Kersee *	7	2.00
McDonald's Jordan/Joyner-Kersee *	8	2.00
North Carolina Collegiate Collection *	3	1.50
North Carolina Collegiate Collection *	44	1.50
North Carolina Collegiate Collection *	61	1.50
North Carolina Collegiate Collection *	89	1.50
North Carolina Collegiate Collection *	93	1.50
North Carolina Collegiate Collection Promos *	NC1	3.50
Panini Stickers	91	2.00
Panini Stickers	G	1.50
Panini Stickers	K	1.50
SkyBox Prototypes	41	50.00
SkyBox	41	3.00

1991-1995 THE WONDER YEARS

SQUEEZE PLAYS

WHEN SUPERSTARS SUCH AS MICHAEL JORDAN AND MAGIC JOHNSON SPRING OUT OF RETIREMENT, CARD COMPANIES ARE SENT SCRAMBLING TO GET THEIR CARDS OUT

When Michael Jordan speaks, everybody listens.

In 1995, when His Airness ended his retirement from basketball and declared, "I'm back," his two-word announcement didn't fall on deaf ears in the hobby. The battle cry of card manufacturers quickly became "hold back," as in "hold back the release date on that set!" as they scrambled to devise last-minute strategies to include Jordan cards in their sets.

From the moment of the first rumor of Jordan's return, basketball card company officials were meeting behind closed doors to map out a way to work the Chicago Bulls superstar into their sets.

And even though Jordan didn't suit up in a game until mid-March — when he ditched No. 23 and showed up in a new jersey number — all of the card manufacturers managed to get cards of Jordan in their late-season issues.

Although he played in just 17 regular season games, Jordan appeared on cards in Flair (#326), Emotion (#100), Topps Embossed (#121), Finest (#331) and Upper Deck SP Championship (#4).

About 10 months later, of course, Magic Johnson pulled off a similar feat by coming back to the Los Angeles Lakers. The interoffice memos circulating at the cardmakers all read the same: Here we go again!

"When you have two major players

BY TOL BROOME

like a Jordan and a Magic coming back, you do everything humanly possible to get them into sets," says Rick Schwartz, Upper Deck's basketball brand manager.

STOP THE PRESSES!

In the case of Jordan, doing "everything humanly possible" ranged from expanding a set by one card to literally stopping the presses. Magic's return also delayed a few releases and, in at least one instance, forced a card company to drop a card of a player off its checklist so that Magic's card could replace it.

"Consumers want to see the latest, greatest cards of players like Michael and Magic," Schwartz says. "You need

Michael Jordan wasn't the only superstar who made a magical comeback after leaving basketball. Less than a year after Jordan returned, Earvin Johnson came out of retirement, too.

new photos and new card backs to make the cards as fresh as possible."

Card manufacturers got creative to squeeze Jordan into their 1994-95 sets. Since he returned wearing uniform No.

45, cardmakers couldn't cheat and use an old photo on his cards. Consequently, nearly every company had photographers focused and flashing away at Jordan's first game back against the Indiana Pacers.

In the eyes of collectors, it was worth the effort. Fleer was able to add Jordan as the last card in its Flair II release and inserted the card at a rate of about one per box. Topps extended its

1991-1995 THE WONDER YEARS

Embossed set from 120 to 121 cards to include a Jordan card. Topps also held up production of its Finest II release just so it could feature a card of Jordan pictured in his No. 45 jersey.

"With Finest, we had to hold up a ship date to get Jordan in that year," explains Topps spokesman Marty Appel.

Working on such short notice, Topps along only once in a lifetime. So it's easy to see why the card companies went to extremes to have his cards grace their sets.

A MAGICAL CHALLENGE

Magic's return earlier this year sent the card companies scrambling for a second consecutive year, although Johnson's comeback in January — in backer.

"Just as Jordan threw us a curve with a new uniform number, Magic presented a challenge with the extra 30 pounds," says Fleer/SkyBox public relations manager Rich Bradley. "We had a photographer at [Magic's] very first game back to ensure access to current photos."

SkyBox was successful in working

treated the Jordan issue like an insert, although it was packaged at the same rate as the set's other regular-issue cards.

"We made him an add-on sheet all by himself," Appel says. "We felt that we are good enough at collation to get his card inserted properly. We treated the Finest Jordan card as though it were an insert, putting it in packs at a normal rate."

A player of Jordan's caliber comes contrast to Jordan's mid-March return — afforded the cardmakers a little more time to figure out how they would get his cards into their sets.

But as was the case with Jordan and his new jersey number, the card companies couldn't simply rely on pulling an old photo of Johnson out of their files. The new Magic came with an extra 30 pounds and an upper body that was more suited for an NFL linean up-to-date Magic card into its Premium Series II release, as well as SkyBox II (#301), Flair II (#11) and Metal II (#161). Insert cards also appear in the Metal Force (#6) and Scoring Magnet (#3) sets found in Fleer Metal II packs. The SkyBox II card was a last-minute addition to a 300-card set, while the Flair II and Metal cards replaced previously planned issues of one of Magic's

THE WONDER YEARS 1991-1995

Lakers teammates — Anthony Peeler.

"Magic's comeback caused Peeler to lose some playing time," Bradley notes. "I guess you could say he ended up losing card time to Magic as well."

Topps also pulled a Lakers player to include Johnson in its Stadium Club Series II release (#361), the same action taken by Upper Deck to put a little Magic into Series II (#237), as well

sport in which he had won three consecutive championships and had dominated so thoroughly, was something that excited even novice collectors. The novelty of his being pictured in a No. 45 jersey only enhanced the lure of his new cards.

"Collectors were really after Jordan's late-season cards last year and still are," says David Green, owner of

as its Special Edition issue. The company commemorated the Magic moment on Johnson's Upper Deck release with a special foil stamp that reads, "Believe in Magic, January 30, 1996."

When Jordan came out of retirement, the anticipation for his cards was as intense as any hobby event in recent history. The world's most famous athlete, returning after 18 months to the

Collectables card shop in Greensboro, N.C.

Initially, Magic's comeback sparked renewed appeal in his cards. His subsequent retirement, on the heels of a disappointing run in the playoffs, has since cooled off much of the hobby interest Magic had generated.

WHEELIN' AND DEALIN'

Superstar comebacks such as those

pulled off by Jordan and Johnson aren't the only NBA trends that wreak havoc on the average basketball card. A rash of trades during the last two seasons has resulted in some players changing cities as often as the Ringling Brothers circus.

And with these moves, the card companies find themselves fighting to keep pace by making sure collectors get what they want — cards of their

favorite players pictured in their most current uniforms. Though not of the same caliber as producing Jordan and Johnson cards late in the season, it's a challenge just the same.

The Miami Heat, for example, changed its entire starting lineup between November and March of 1996 following a series of trades that saw Glen Rice, Matt Geiger, Khalid Reeves, Kevin Willis and Billy Owens leave town, only to be replaced by Alonzo Mourning, Tim Hardaway, Walt Williams and Chris Gatling.

Elsewhere around the NBA, such recognizable players who changed addresses during the '95-96 season included Derrick Coleman, Kenny Anderson, Shawn Bradley, Kendall Gill, Christian Laettner, Charles Smith and B.J. Armstrong.

Salary cap considerations have led

It's gotta be the shoes, right? While players such as Shawn Bradley change teams more often than they change socks, Jordan won six championships for one club.

some teams to deal perfectly good players to make room under the salary cap. Also, some teams seem to be giving up on players more quickly than in the past. And, of course, teams always are looking to improve.

"Teams are always trying to be more

When it comes to late-season roster additions, it's usually worth a card company's time and money to make sure a player of Jordan's caliber gets into a set with his new uniform that same year.

flexible," says Los Angeles Lakers president Jerry West, who was never traded during his 14-season career with the Lakers. "They want a piece of a puzzle to make their teams better, and

they look to deals with other teams to try and accomplish that."

In light of all the trades that have occurred the last two seasons, card company design teams often have found themselves scrambling to beat the buzzer in their efforts to obtain updated photography of players with their new teams.

"We want to have the freshest set possible," Schwartz says. "Nobody

1991-1995 THE WONDER YEARS

likes to release a set with a player pictured in the wrong uniform who has been traded."

Through the years, Upper Deck has adjusted to trades in several ways:

• Trades that occur early enough in the season usually allow the company to include the key players pictured with their new teams in its Series II products.

• In its '95-96 Collector's Choice

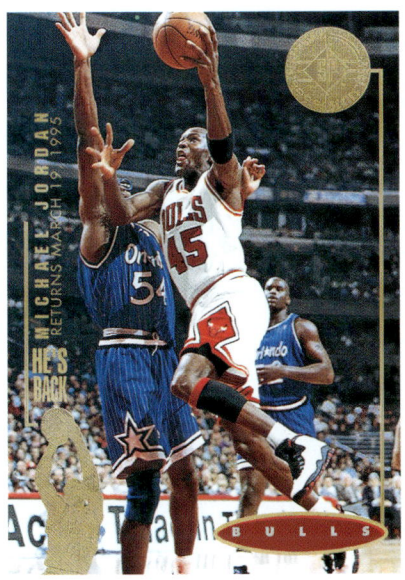

set, Upper Deck created a mail-in program in which an inserted card can be redeemed for a special "traded" set — capturing all the key players who were traded throughout the season with their new teams.

• Foil stamps on the front of cards also are utilized as a way to indicate that a player has been traded, even though some players may be pictured on the card in their old uniform.

• Late-season release dates for such sets as SP Championship allow Upper Deck more flexibility in acquiring photos of players in their current uniforms.

Within the hallways of the Topps offices, decisions regarding the inclusion of traded players in the company's various sets generally are based on three factors: 1) release date of the set; 2) date of the trade; and 3) caliber of the player traded.

With most Topps sets, if a trade occurs before December, there usually is enough time to include the player with his new team in Series II issues. If a trade occurs near the league's trading deadline in late February, the players probably won't appear on a card in their new uniforms until the following year's sets are released.

DEADLINE DECISIONS

And what happens when two general managers pull off a trade in January or early February? Then Topps must factor in the player's star power.

"There comes a time when you say this is the cutoff and whatever we have, we have," Appel says. "If it's a player who can clearly make a difference, who can drive sales of the product, then you can make an extraordinary effort. As far as trades, there really were none this year that warranted that kind of effort."

Bradley says Fleer/SkyBox also decided there were no superstar players involved in late-season trades in '95-96 who warranted holding back release dates.

"Most of the early trades were taken care of in Series II," Bradley says, adding that Flair II includes cards of Coleman with the 76ers, Bradley with the Nets and Mourning (who also appears in Flair Series I with the Hornets) with the Heat.

"Later trades like the trading deadline deals won't be reflected until Series I of next year in most cases," says Bradley, who notes that Fleer/SkyBox is considering adjusting launch dates for some Series II releases in the future to better react to trades. "No real big names moved in later trades. There was no major uprising in the hobby to get the first card of Christian Laettner in an Atlanta Hawks uniform."

Maybe not. But when it comes to the game's true superstars such as Jordan and Johnson, collectors can be sure the card manufacturers will stop at nothing — including stopping the presses — to deliver the cards the hobby wants most.

Tol Broome is a freelance writer in Greensboro, N.C.

1991-1995 THE WONDER YEARS

PRICE GUIDE

Basketball Cards

1991-92 through 1994-95

Values were full retail selling prices at the time of publication, but it should be noted that lower prices can be found through extensive shopping. Cards from 1989-90 to present are valued in Mint, characterized by 60/40 or better centering, smooth edges, original color borders and gloss, and no print spots and color or focus imperfections. * denotes a multisport set.

THE WONDER YEARS 1991-1995

1991-92

Set	No.	Price
5 Majeur	21D	40.00
5 Majeur	28E	50.00
Arena Holograms 12th National *	3	5.00
Cleo Michael Jordan Valentines	1	.75
Cleo Michael Jordan Valentines	2	.75
Cleo Michael Jordan Valentines	3	.75
Cleo Michael Jordan Valentines	4	.75
Cleo Michael Jordan Valentines	5	.75
Cleo Michael Jordan Valentines	6	.75
Cleo Michael Jordan Valentines	7	.75
Cleo Michael Jordan Valentines	8	.75
Cleo Michael Jordan Valentines	9	.75
Cleo Michael Jordan Valentines	10	.75
Cleo Michael Jordan Valentines	11	.75
Farley's Fruit Snacks	1	3.00
Farley's Fruit Snacks	2	3.00
Farley's Fruit Snacks	3	3.00
Farley's Fruit Snacks	4	3.00
Fleer	29	2.00
Fleer	211	1.00
Fleer	220	1.00
Fleer	233	.50
Fleer	237	.25
Fleer	238	.50
Fleer	375	1.00
Fleer Pro-Visions	2	3.00
Fleer Tony's Pizza	33	50.00
Fleer Wheaties Sheets	6	30.00
Hoops Prototypes 00	4	50.00
Hoops 100 Superstars	13	15.00
Hoops	30	3.00
Hoops	253	1.50
Hoops	306	1.00
Hoops	317	1.50
Hoops	455	1.50
Hoops	536	1.50
Hoops	542	1.50
Hoops	543	1.50
Hoops	579	6.00
Hoops All-Star MVP's	9	15.00
Hoops Slam Dunk	4	15.00
Hoops McDonald's	5	4.00
Hoops McDonald's	55	4.00
Hoops Team Night Sheets	4A	8.00
Hoops Team Night Sheets	4B	8.00
Little Basketball Big Leaguers	19	10.00
Nike Michael Jordan/Spike Lee	1	1.50
Nike Michael Jordan/Spike Lee	2	1.00
Nike Michael Jordan/Spike Lee	3	1.00
Nike Michael Jordan/Spike Lee	4	1.00
Nike Michael Jordan/Spike Lee	5	1.00
Nike Michael Jordan/Spike Lee	6	1.50
Panini Stickers	96	2.50
Panini Stickers	116	5.00
Panini Stickers	190	2.50
Pro Set Prototypes	4	600.00
Pro Stars Posters	2	3.00
SkyBox	39	5.00
SkyBox	307	2.50
SkyBox	333	2.00
SkyBox	334	2.50
SkyBox	337	1.25
SkyBox	408	2.50
SkyBox	462	1.50
SkyBox	534	10.00
SkyBox	572	2.50
SkyBox	583	2.50
SkyBox Canadian Minis	7	6.00
SkyBox Mark and See Minis	534	10.00
SkyBox Mark and See Minis	545	3.00
Upper Deck Promos	1	15.00
Upper Deck	22	.75
Upper Deck	34	1.00
Upper Deck	44	3.00
Upper Deck	48	1.50
Upper Deck	69	1.50
Upper Deck	75	1.50
Upper Deck	452	3.00
Upper Deck Award Winner Holograms	AW1	12.00
Upper Deck Award Winner Holograms	AW4	12.00

1991-1995 THE WONDER YEARS

Set	No.	Price
Upper Deck Sheets	6	20.00
Upper Deck Sheets	14	20.00
Wooden Award Winners	13	3.00

1992-93

Set	No.	Price
ACC Tournament Champs	29	20.00
Fleer	32	3.00
Fleer	238	1.50
Fleer	246	1.50
Fleer	273	1.50
Fleer All-Stars	6	50.00
Fleer Team Leaders	4	150.00
Fleer Total D	5	50.00
Fleer Drake's	7	30.00
Fleer Team Night Sheets	3	15.00
Fleer Tony's Pizza	89	20.00
Hoops	30	3.00
Hoops	298	1.50
Hoops	320	1.00
Hoops	341	1.50
Hoops	TR1	3.00
Hoops Supreme Court	SC1	20.00
Hoops 100 Superstars	14	25.00
Impel U.S. Olympic Hopefuls	12	3.00
Panini Stickers	12	2.00
Panini Stickers	16	.75
Panini Stickers	17	.75
Panini Stickers	18	.75
Panini Stickers	19	.75
Panini Stickers	20	2.00
Panini Stickers	102	2.00
Panini Stickers	128	4.00
SkyBox	31	6.00
SkyBox	314	3.00
SkyBox Olympic Team	11	25.00
SkyBox School Ties	ST16	12.00
SkyBox USA	37	1.50
SkyBox USA	38	1.50
SkyBox USA	39	1.50
SkyBox USA	40	1.50
SkyBox USA	41	1.50
SkyBox USA	42	1.50
SkyBox USA	43	1.50
SkyBox USA	44	1.50
SkyBox USA	45	1.50
SkyBox USA	105	1.50
Sports Illustrated for Kids II	4	20.00
Sports Illustrated for Kids II	374	8.00
Sports Illustrated for Kids II	571	.50
Stadium Club	1	8.00
Stadium Club	210	4.00
Stadium Club Beam Team	1	70.00
Stadium Club Members Only	1	30.00
Stadium Club Members Only	210	15.00
Stadium Club Members Only	BT1	40.00
Topps	3	1.00
Topps	115	1.00
Topps	141	2.00
Topps	205	1.00
Topps Gold	3G	5.00
Topps Gold	115G	5.00
Topps Gold	141G	10.00
Topps Gold	205G	5.00
Topps Beam Team	3	5.00
Topps Beam Team Gold	3	75.00
Topps Archives	52	4.00
Topps Archives Gold	52G	20.00
Ultra	27	6.00
Ultra	216	2.00
Ultra	NNO	2.50
Ultra All-NBA	4	25.00
Ultra Award Winners	1	25.00
Upper Deck	23	4.00
Upper Deck	62	1.00
Upper Deck	67	2.00
Upper Deck	425	2.00
Upper Deck	453A	20.00
Upper Deck	453B	2.00
Upper Deck	488	2.00

MICHAEL JORDAN COLLECTIBLES 47

THE WONDER YEARS 1991-1995

Set	No.	Price
Upper Deck	506	2.00
Upper Deck	510	1.00
Upper Deck	SP2	8.00
Upper Deck All-Division	AD9	10.00
Upper Deck All-NBA	AN1	30.00
Upper Deck Award Winner Holograms	AW1	15.00
Upper Deck Award Winner Holograms	AW9	15.00
Upper Deck 15000 Point Club	PC4	30.00
Upper Deck European	4	1.50
Upper Deck European	38	3.00
Upper Deck European	107	1.50
Upper Deck European	158	1.50
Upper Deck European	166	.60
Upper Deck European	172	1.50
Upper Deck European	174	.75
Upper Deck European	176	1.50
Upper Deck European	177	1.50
Upper Deck European	178	1.50
Upper Deck European	181	1.50
Upper Deck European Award Winner Holograms	2	6.00
Upper Deck European Award Winner Holograms	3	6.00
Upper Deck Team MVPs	TM1	25.00
Upper Deck Team MVPs	TM5	25.00
Upper Deck Jerry West Selects	JW1	20.00
Upper Deck Jerry West Selects	JW4	20.00
Upper Deck Jerry West Selects	JW8	20.00
Upper Deck Jerry West Selects	JW9	20.00
Upper Deck McDonald's	P5	3.00
Upper Deck McDonald's	CH4	10.00
Upper Deck McDonald's	NNO	10.00
Upper Deck All-Star Weekend	15	3.00
Upper Deck MVP Holograms	4	10.00
Upper Deck Sheets	8	25.00

1993-94

Set	No.	Price
Fax Pax World of Sport *	7	4.00
Finest	1	20.00
Finest Refractors	1	300.00
Fleer	28	3.00
Fleer	224	1.50
Fleer All-Stars	5	30.00
Fleer Living Legends	4	20.00
Fleer NBA Superstars	7	10.00
Fleer Sharpshooters	3	25.00
Hoops	28	3.00
Hoops	257	1.50
Hoops	283	.75
Hoops	289	.75
Hoops Fifth Anniversary Gold	28	8.00
Hoops Fifth Anniversary Gold	257	4.00
Hoops Fifth Anniversary Gold	283	2.00
Hoops Fifth Anniversary Gold	289	2.00
Hoops Face to Face	10	15.00
Hoops Supreme Court	SC11	6.00
Jam Session	33	6.00
McDonald's Nothing But Net MVPs	#4	8
Nike/Warner Michael Jordan	1	1.00
Nike/Warner Michael Jordan	2	1.00
Nike/Warner Michael Jordan	3	1.00
Nike/Warner Michael Jordan	4	2.00
Nike/Warner Michael Jordan	5	2.00
Nike/Warner Michael Jordan	6	1.00
Nike/Warner Michael Jordan	7	2.00
Nike/Warner Michael Jordan	8	1.00
Nike/Warner Michael Jordan	9	1.00
Nike/Warner Michael Jordan	10	2.00
Nike/Warner Michael Jordan	11	1.00
Nike/Warner Michael Jordan	12	1.00
SkyBox Promos	1	10.00
SkyBox	14	2.00
SkyBox	45	4.00
SkyBox Center Stage	CS1	25.00
SkyBox Dynamic Dunks	D4	20.00
SkyBox Showdown Series	SS11	2.00
Stadium Club	1	2.50
Stadium Club	169	5.00
Stadium Club	181	2.00
Stadium Club First Day Issue	1	60.00
Stadium Club First Day Issue	169	125.00
Stadium Club First Day Issue	181	50.00

1991-1995 THE WONDER YEARS

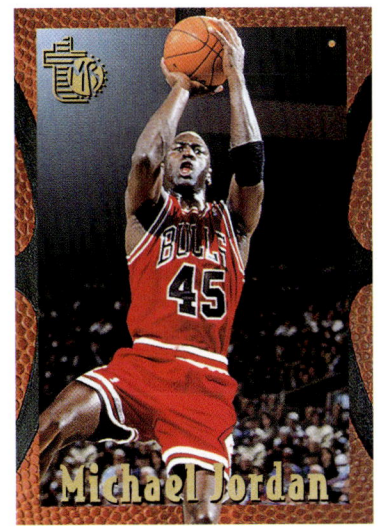

Set	No.	Price
Stadium Club Beam Team	4	20.00
Stadium Club Super Teams NBA Finals	1	6.00
Stadium Club Super Teams NBA Finals	169	12.00
Stadium Club Super Teams NBA Finals	181	6.00
Stadium Club Members Only	1	12.00
Stadium Club Members Only	169	25.00
Stadium Club Members Only	181	12.00
Stadium Club Members Only	BT4	25.00
Stadium Club Members Only 59	6	8.00
Topps	23	3.00
Topps	64	1.50
Topps	101	1.50
Topps	199	1.50
Topps	384	1.50
Topps Gold	23G	12.00
Topps Gold	64G	6.00
Topps Gold	101G	6.00
Topps Gold	199G	6.00
Topps Gold	384G	6.00
Ultra	30	4.00
Ultra All-Defensive	2	100.00
Ultra All-NBA	2	30.00
Ultra All-Rookie Team	2	1.50
Ultra Famous Nicknames	7	25.00
Ultra Inside/Outside	4	8.00
Ultra Power In The Key	2	40.00
Ultra Scoring Kings	5	80.00
Upper Deck	23	4.00
Upper Deck	166	2.00
Upper Deck	171	2.00
Upper Deck	180	1.00
Upper Deck	187	1.00
Upper Deck	193	2.00
Upper Deck	198	2.00
Upper Deck	201	2.00
Upper Deck	204	2.00
Upper Deck	213	1.00
Upper Deck	237	2.00
Upper Deck	438	2.00
Upper Deck	466	2.00
Upper Deck	SP3	8.00
Upper Deck All-NBA	AN4	8.00
Upper Deck All-NBA	AN15	4.00
Upper Deck Box Bottoms	2	2.00
Upper Deck European	5	2.00
Upper Deck European	33	2.00
Upper Deck European	43	2.00
Upper Deck European	86	2.00
Upper Deck European	90	2.50
Upper Deck European	118	4.00
Upper Deck European Award Winner Holograms	1	8.00
Upper Deck European Award Winner Holograms	9	8.00
Upper Deck French McDonald's	15	15.00
Upper Deck Holojams	H4	12.00
Upper Deck Locker Talk	LT1	40.00
Upper Deck Mr. June	MJ1	20.00
Upper Deck Mr. June	MJ2	20.00
Upper Deck Mr. June	MJ3	20.00
Upper Deck Mr. June	MJ4	20.00
Upper Deck Mr. June	MJ5	20.00
Upper Deck Mr. June	MJ6	20.00
Upper Deck Mr. June	MJ7	20.00
Upper Deck Mr. June	MJ8	20.00
Upper Deck Mr. June	MJ9	20.00
Upper Deck Pro View	23	4.00
Upper Deck Pro View	91	2.00
Upper Deck SE	MJR1	10.00
Upper Deck SE Behind the Glass	G11	25.00
Upper Deck SE USA Trade	5	25.00
Upper Deck Sheets	1	10.00
Upper Deck Triple Double	TD2	15.00

1994-95

Set	No.	Price
Basketball USA	26	75.00
Bleachers 23 Karat Gold	8	50.00
Bleachers 23 Karat Gold	9	50.00
Bleachers 23 Karat Gold	10	40.00
Bleachers 23 Karat Gold	11	50.00
Bleachers 23 Karat Gold	12	60.00
Collector's Choice	23	2.50
Collector's Choice	204	1.25

THE WONDER YEARS 1991-1995

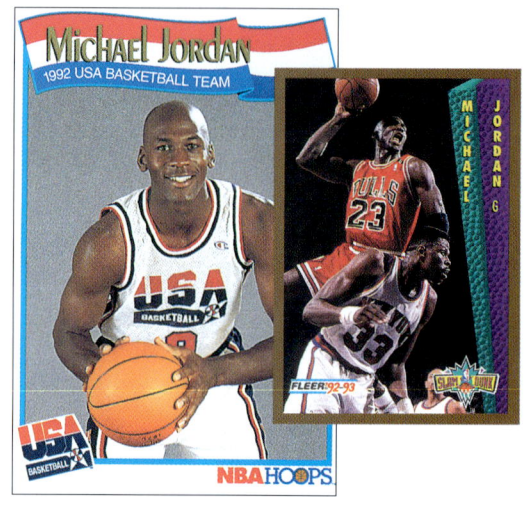

Card	Number	Price
Collector's Choice	240	1.25
Collector's Choice	402	1.25
Collector's Choice	420	.75
Collector's Choice Blow-Ups	23	8.00
Collector's Choice Blow-Ups Autograph	A23	5000.00
Collector's Choice Gold Signature	23	100.00
Collector's Choice Gold Signature	204	50.00
Collector's Choice Gold Signature	240	50.00
Collector's Choice Gold Signature	402	50.00
Collector's Choice Gold Signature	420	30.00
Collector's Choice Silver Signature	23	8.00
Collector's Choice Silver Signature	204	4.00
Collector's Choice Silver Signature	240	4.00
Collector's Choice Silver Signature	402	4.00
Collector's Choice Silver Signature	420	2.00
Embossed	121	10.00
Embossed Golden Idols	121	25.00
Emotion	100	12.00
Emotion N-Tense	N3	50.00
Finest	331	25.00
Finest Refractors	331	400.00
Flair	326	15.00
SP	P23	15.00
SP	MJ1R	6.00
SP	MJ1S	25.00
SP Championship	4	4.00
SP Championship	41	8.00
SP Championship Die Cuts	4	10.00
SP Championship Die Cuts	41	20.00
SP Championship Playoff Heroes	P2	30.00
SP Championship Playoff Heroes Die Cuts	P2	150.00
Upper Deck	359	2.50
Upper Deck European	23	3.00
Upper Deck European	166	4.00
Upper Deck European	167	4.00
Upper Deck European	168	4.00
Upper Deck European	169	4.00
Upper Deck European	170	4.00
Upper Deck European	171	4.00
Upper Deck European	172	4.00
Upper Deck European	173	4.00
Upper Deck European	174	4.00
Upper Deck European	175	4.00
Upper Deck European	176	3.00
Upper Deck European Triple Double	TD2	10.00
Upper Deck French McDonald's Team	4	4.00
Upper Deck French McDonald's Team	29H	100.00
Upper Deck Jordan He's Back Reprints	23	1.50
Upper Deck Jordan He's Back Reprints	23	1.50
Upper Deck Jordan He's Back Reprints	41	1.50
Upper Deck Jordan He's Back Reprints	44	1.50
Upper Deck Jordan He's Back Reprints	204	1.50
Upper Deck Jordan He's Back Reprints	237	1.50
Upper Deck Jordan He's Back Reprints	402	1.50
Upper Deck Jordan He's Back Reprints	425	1.50
Upper Deck Jordan He's Back Reprints	453	1.50
Upper Deck Jordan He's Back Reprints	J1	5.00
Upper Deck Jordan He's Back Reprints	J2	5.00
Upper Deck Jordan He's Back Reprints	J3	5.00
Upper Deck Jordan Heroes	37	10.00
Upper Deck Jordan Heroes	38	10.00
Upper Deck Jordan Heroes	39	10.00
Upper Deck Jordan Heroes	40	10.00
Upper Deck Jordan Heroes	41	10.00
Upper Deck Jordan Heroes	42	10.00
Upper Deck Jordan Heroes	43	10.00
Upper Deck Jordan Heroes	44	10.00
Upper Deck Jordan Heroes	45	10.00
Upper Deck Jordan Heroes	NNO	10.00
Upper Deck Jordan Rare Air	1	1.00
Upper Deck Jordan Rare Air	2	1.00
Upper Deck Jordan Rare Air	3	.50
Upper Deck Jordan Rare Air	4	.25
Upper Deck Jordan Rare Air	5	.50
Upper Deck Jordan Rare Air	6	.50
Upper Deck Jordan Rare Air	7	.50
Upper Deck Jordan Rare Air	8	.50
Upper Deck Jordan Rare Air	9	.50
Upper Deck Jordan Rare Air	10	.50
Upper Deck Jordan Rare Air	11	.50
Upper Deck Jordan Rare Air	12	.50
Upper Deck Jordan Rare Air	13	.25
Upper Deck Jordan Rare Air	14	.50
Upper Deck Jordan Rare Air	15	.25
Upper Deck Jordan Rare Air	16	1.00
Upper Deck Jordan Rare Air	17	.50
Upper Deck Jordan Rare Air	18	1.00
Upper Deck Jordan Rare Air	19	.50

EVERYTHING YOU NEED TO KNOW ABOUT

1991-1995 THE WONDER YEARS

Card	No.	Price
Upper Deck Jordan Rare Air	20	.50
Upper Deck Jordan Rare Air	21	.25
Upper Deck Jordan Rare Air	22	1.00
Upper Deck Jordan Rare Air	23	1.00
Upper Deck Jordan Rare Air	24	.50
Upper Deck Jordan Rare Air	25	.50
Upper Deck Jordan Rare Air	26	.50
Upper Deck Jordan Rare Air	27	.25
Upper Deck Jordan Rare Air	28	.50
Upper Deck Jordan Rare Air	29	.50
Upper Deck Jordan Rare Air	30	.50
Upper Deck Jordan Rare Air	31	.50
Upper Deck Jordan Rare Air	32	.50
Upper Deck Jordan Rare Air	33	1.00
Upper Deck Jordan Rare Air	34	1.00
Upper Deck Jordan Rare Air	35	.25
Upper Deck Jordan Rare Air	36	.50
Upper Deck Jordan Rare Air	37	1.00
Upper Deck Jordan Rare Air	38	1.00
Upper Deck Jordan Rare Air	39	.50
Upper Deck Jordan Rare Air	40	.50
Upper Deck Jordan Rare Air	41	.50
Upper Deck Jordan Rare Air	42	.50
Upper Deck Jordan Rare Air	43	.50
Upper Deck Jordan Rare Air	44	.50
Upper Deck Jordan Rare Air	45	.50
Upper Deck Jordan Rare Air	46	1.00
Upper Deck Jordan Rare Air	47	.50
Upper Deck Jordan Rare Air	48	1.00
Upper Deck Jordan Rare Air	49	.25
Upper Deck Jordan Rare Air	50	1.00
Upper Deck Jordan Rare Air	51	.25
Upper Deck Jordan Rare Air	52	.25
Upper Deck Jordan Rare Air	53	.50
Upper Deck Jordan Rare Air	54	.50
Upper Deck Jordan Rare Air	55	.50
Upper Deck Jordan Rare Air	56	.50
Upper Deck Jordan Rare Air	57	.50
Upper Deck Jordan Rare Air	58	.50
Upper Deck Jordan Rare Air	59	.50
Upper Deck Jordan Rare Air	60	.50
Upper Deck Jordan Rare Air	61	1.00
Upper Deck Jordan Rare Air	62	1.00
Upper Deck Jordan Rare Air	63	1.00
Upper Deck Jordan Rare Air	64	1.00
Upper Deck Jordan Rare Air	65	1.00
Upper Deck Jordan Rare Air	66	.50
Upper Deck Jordan Rare Air	67	.50
Upper Deck Jordan Rare Air	68	.50
Upper Deck Jordan Rare Air	69	.50
Upper Deck Jordan Rare Air	70	.50
Upper Deck Jordan Rare Air	71	.50
Upper Deck Jordan Rare Air	72	1.00
Upper Deck Jordan Rare Air	73	.50
Upper Deck Jordan Rare Air	74	.50
Upper Deck Jordan Rare Air	75	1.00
Upper Deck Jordan Rare Air	76	1.00
Upper Deck Jordan Rare Air	77	.50
Upper Deck Jordan Rare Air	78	1.00
Upper Deck Jordan Rare Air	79	.50
Upper Deck Jordan Rare Air	80	.50
Upper Deck Jordan Rare Air	81	.50
Upper Deck Jordan Rare Air	82	.50
Upper Deck Jordan Rare Air	83	1.00
Upper Deck Jordan Rare Air	84	.50
Upper Deck Jordan Rare Air	85	1.00
Upper Deck Jordan Rare Air	86	.50
Upper Deck Jordan Rare Air	87	.50
Upper Deck Jordan Rare Air	88	.50
Upper Deck Jordan Rare Air	89	1.00
Upper Deck Jordan Rare Air	90	.50
Upper Deck Jordan Rare Air	NNO	1.00
Upper Deck Jordan Rare Air	NNO	1.00
Upper Deck Nothing But Net	1	1.00
Upper Deck Nothing But Net	5	1.50
Upper Deck Nothing But Net	7	1.00
Upper Deck Nothing But Net	9	1.00
Upper Deck Nothing But Net	12	1.00
Upper Deck Nothing But Net	13	1.50
Upper Deck USA	85	2.50
Upper Deck USA Gold Medal	85	10.00
Upper Deck USA Jordan's Highlights	JH1	10.00
Upper Deck USA Jordan's Highlights	JH2	10.00
Upper Deck USA Jordan's Highlights	JH3	10.00
Upper Deck USA Jordan's Highlights	JH4	10.00
Upper Deck USA Jordan's Highlights	JH5	10.00
Upper Deck Sheets	3	10.00

1995-1999 THE GOLDEN YEARS

Jordan's Grand Babies

AND WE'RE NOT TALKING ABOUT HIS CHILDREN'S CHILDREN, EITHER!

In the grand scheme of things, it comes down to this: Nine pieces of cardboard at an average cost of $3,522.22 per.

Sure, the cardboard may have Jordan's signature attached . . . or a piece of his jersey . . . or a signature piece of his jersey . . . or Refractor technology. But it's nine pieces of cardboard nonetheless.

Nine pieces of cardboard for $31,700 — that's the composite value of Jordan's '97-98 cards that booked for $1,000 or more in the September issue of *Beckett Basketball Card Monthly* (#98).

You know what else you could get for $31,700? Try 26 autographed jerseys from Upper Deck Authenticated. Try 31 Fleer Rookies — with $700 left to spare. Try 10 1984-85 Jordan

By Tracy Hackler

Star XRCs; heck, try six complete '84-85 Star sets.

Goodness, you could rent a $500-a-month studio apartment for storage of your MJ collection for 63 months.

But what the hey, if you've got an extra 30 grand to toss around — and who of us doesn't? — the following nine cards are a great place to start.

Tracy Hackler is an editor at Beckett Publications.

THE GOLDEN YEARS — 1995-1999

1 1997-98 Upper Deck Game Jersey Autograph #GJ13S $10,000

2 1997-98 Metal Universe Precious Metal Gems Green #23 $8,500

3 1997-98 Upper Deck Game Jersey #GJ13 $2,500

4 1997-98 Upper Deck UD3 Season Ticket Autograph #MJ $2,500

5 1997-98 SkyBox Star Rubies #29 $2,000

1995-1999 THE GOLDEN YEARS

6 1997-98 Finest Embossed Refractor Gold #154 $1,800

7 1997-98 SkyBox Star Rubies #235 $1,600

8 1997-98 SkyBox Z-Force Super Rave #190 $1,500

9 1997-98 Skybox E-X2001 Essential Credentials Future #9 $1,200

MICHAEL JORDAN COLLECTIBLES   **55**

1995-1999 THE GOLDEN YEARS

Price Guide

Basketball Cards

1995-96 through 1998-99

Values were full retail selling prices at the time of publication, but it should be noted that lower prices can be found through extensive shopping. Cards from 1989-90 to present are valued in Mint, characterized by 60/40 or better centering, smooth edges, original color borders and gloss, and no print spots and color or focus imperfections. * denotes a multisport set.

THE GOLDEN YEARS 1995-1999

1995-96

Set	No.	Price
Collector's Choice	45	2.50
Collector's Choice	169	1.25
Collector's Choice	173	.75
Collector's Choice	195	1.25
Collector's Choice	210	.60
Collector's Choice	324	1.25
Collector's Choice	353	1.25
Collector's Choice	410	.60
Collector's Choice Player's Club	45	8.00
Collector's Choice Player's Club	169	4.00
Collector's Choice Player's Club	173	2.00
Collector's Choice Player's Club	195	4.00
Collector's Choice Player's Club	210	2.00
Collector's Choice Player's Club	324	4.00
Collector's Choice Player's Club	353	4.00
Collector's Choice Player's Club	410	2.00
Collector's Choice Player's Club Platinum	45	75.00
Collector's Choice Player's Club Platinum	169	40.00
Collector's Choice Player's Club Platinum	173	20.00
Collector's Choice Player's Club Platinum	195	40.00
Collector's Choice Player's Club Platinum	210	20.00
Collector's Choice Player's Club Platinum	324	40.00
Collector's Choice Player's Club Platinum	353	40.00
Collector's Choice Player's Club Platinum	410	20.00
Collector's Choice Crash the Game Assists/Rebounds	C1	8.00
Collector's Choice Crash the Game Assists/Rebounds	C1B	8.00
Collector's Choice Crash the Game Assists/Rebounds	C1C	8.00
Collector's Choice Crash the Game Assists/Rebounds Gold	C1	30.00
Collector's Choice Crash the Game Assists/Rebounds Gold	C1B	30.00
Collector's Choice Crash the Game Assists/Rebounds Gold	C1C	30.00
Collector's Choice Crash the Game Assists/Rebounds Silver Redemption	C1	4.00
Collector's Choice Crash the Game Assists/Rebounds Gold Redemption	C1	15.00
Collector's Choice Crash the Game Scoring	C1	8.00
Collector's Choice Crash the Game Scoring	C1B	8.00
Collector's Choice Crash the Game Scoring	C1C	8.00
Collector's Choice Crash the Game Scoring Gold	C1	30.00
Collector's Choice Crash the Game Scoring Gold	C1B	30.00
Collector's Choice Crash the Game Scoring Gold	C1C	30.00
Collector's Choice Crash the Game Scoring Silver Redemption	C1	4.00
Collector's Choice Crash the Game Scoring Silver Redemption	XC30	4.00
Collector's Choice Crash the Game Scoring Gold Redemption	C1	15.00
Collector's Choice Crash the Game Scoring Gold Redemption	XC30	15.00
Collector's Choice Jordan He's Back	M1	1.50
Collector's Choice Jordan He's Back	M2	1.50
Collector's Choice Jordan He's Back	M3	1.50
Collector's Choice Jordan He's Back	M4	1.50
Collector's Choice Jordan He's Back	M5	1.50
Collector's Choice Jordan Collection	JC1	3.00
Collector's Choice Jordan Collection	JC2	3.00
Collector's Choice Jordan Collection	JC3	3.00
Collector's Choice Jordan Collection	JC4	3.00
Collector's Choice Jordan Collection	JC9	3.00
Collector's Choice Jordan Collection	JC10	3.00
Collector's Choice Jordan Collection	JC11	3.00
Collector's Choice Jordan Collection	JC12	3.00
Collector's Choice European Stickers	120	10.00
Collector's Choice European Stickers	MJ1	4.00
Collector's Choice European Stickers	MJ2	4.00
Collector's Choice European Stickers	MJ3	4.00
Collector's Choice European Stickers	MJ4	4.00
Collector's Choice European Stickers	MJ5	4.00
Collector's Choice European Stickers	MJ6	4.00
Collector's Choice European Stickers	MJ7	4.00
Collector's Choice European Stickers	MJ8	4.00

1995-1999 THE GOLDEN YEARS

Item	Number	Price
Collector's Choice European Stickers	MJ9	4.00
Collector's Choice Int'l European	23	3.00
Collector's Choice Int'l European	204	1.50
Collector's Choice Int'l European	211	6.00
Collector's Choice Int'l European	212	6.00
Collector's Choice Int'l European	213	6.00
Collector's Choice Int'l European	214	6.00
Collector's Choice Int'l European	215	6.00
Collector's Choice Int'l European	216	6.00
Collector's Choice Int'l European	217	6.00
Collector's Choice Int'l European	218	6.00
Collector's Choice Int'l European	219	6.00
Collector's Choice Int'l European	240	1.50
Collector's Choice Int'l European	402	1.50
Collector's Choice Int'l European	420	.75
Collector's Choice Int'l European Gold Signatures	402	15.00
Collector's Choice Int'l Japanese I	23	10.00
Collector's Choice Int'l Japanese I	204	5.00
Collector's Choice Int'l Japanese I	211	15.00
Collector's Choice Int'l Japanese I	212	15.00
Collector's Choice Int'l Japanese I	213	15.00
Collector's Choice Int'l Japanese I	214	15.00
Collector's Choice Int'l Japanese I	215	15.00
Collector's Choice Int'l Japanese I	216	15.00
Collector's Choice Int'l Japanese I	217	15.00
Collector's Choice Int'l Japanese I	218	15.00
Collector's Choice Int'l Japanese I	219	15.00
Collector's Choice Int'l Japanese II	240	5.00
Collector's Choice Int'l Japanese II	402	5.00
Collector's Choice Int'l Japanese II	420	2.50
Collector's Choice Int'l Japanese Gold Signatures II	402	80.00
Collector's Choice Int'l Spanish I	23	3.00
Collector's Choice Int'l Spanish I	204	1.50
Collector's Choice Int'l Spanish I	211	3.00
Collector's Choice Int'l Spanish I	212	3.00
Collector's Choice Int'l Spanish I	213	3.00
Collector's Choice Int'l Spanish I	214	3.00
Collector's Choice Int'l Spanish I	215	3.00
Collector's Choice Int'l Spanish I	216	3.00
Collector's Choice Int'l Spanish I	217	3.00
Collector's Choice Int'l Spanish I	218	3.00
Collector's Choice Int'l Spanish I	219	3.00
Collector's Choice Intl Spanish II	21	1.50
Collector's Choice Intl Spanish II	183	1.50
Collector's Choice Intl Spanish II	201	.75
Collector's Choice Int'l Decade of Dominance	J1	4.00
Collector's Choice Int'l Decade of Dominance	J2	4.00
Collector's Choice Int'l Decade of Dominance	J3	4.00
Collector's Choice Int'l Decade of Dominance	J4	4.00
Collector's Choice Int'l Decade of Dominance	J5	4.00
Collector's Choice Int'l Decade of Dominance	J6	4.00
Collector's Choice Int'l Decade of Dominance	J7	4.00
Collector's Choice Int'l Decade of Dominance	J8	4.00
Collector's Choice Int'l Decade of Dominance	J9	4.00
Collector's Choice Int'l Decade of Dominance	J10	4.00
Finest	229	15.00
Finest Refractors	229	350.00
Finest Dish and Swish	DS4	100.00
Finest Hot Stuff	HS1	25.00
Finest Mystery	M1	12.00
Finest Mystery Bordered Refractors Test	M1	5000.00
Finest Mystery Borderless/Silver	M1	60.00
Finest Mystery Borderless Refractors/Gold	M1	350.00
Finest Veteran/Rookie	RV20	100.00
Flair	15	12.00
Flair	235	4.00
Flair Anticipation	2	60.00
Flair Hot Numbers	4	80.00
Flair New Heights	4	40.00
Fleer	22	3.00
Fleer	323	1.50
Fleer End to End	9	10.00
Fleer Flair Hardwood Leaders	4	8.00
Fleer Total D	3	8.00
Fleer Total O	2	25.00
Fleer Total O Hot Pack	2	15.00
Hoop Magazine/Mother's Cookies	4	25.00
Hoops	21	3.00
Hoops	358	1.50
Hoops Hot List	1	25.00

THE GOLDEN YEARS 1995-1999

Card	Number	Price
Hoops Number Crunchers	1	5.00
Hoops Power Palette	1	25.00
Hoops Sheets	3	5.00
Hoops SkyView	SV1	60.00
Hoops Top Ten	AR7	20.00
Jam Session	13	5.00
Jam Session Die Cuts	D13	12.00
Jam Session Show Stoppers	3	125.00
Metal	13	6.00
Metal	212	2.50
Metal Silver Spotlight	13	20.00
Metal Maximum Metal	4	40.00
Metal Scoring Magnets	4	60.00
Metal Slick Silver	3	25.00
Metal Stackhouse's Scrapbook	S7	8.00
Panini Stickers	83	5.00
SkyBox	15	4.00
SkyBox	278	2.00
SkyBox Larger Than Life	L1	60.00
SkyBox Meltdown	M1	50.00
SkyBox Standouts Hobby	SH1	50.00
SkyBox E-XL	10	8.00
Skybox E-XL Blue	10	20.00
SkyBox E-XL Natural Born Thrillers	1	100.00
SkyBox E-XL No Boundaries	1	50.00
SP	23	5.00
SP All-Stars	AS2	20.00
SP All-Stars Gold	AS2	150.00
SP Holoviews	PC5	30.00
SP Holoview Die Cuts	PC5	120.00
SP Jordan Collection	JC17	12.00
SP Jordan Collection	JC18	12.00
SP Jordan Collection	JC19	12.00
SP Jordan Collection	JC20	12.00
SP Championship	17	5.00
SP Championship	121	2.50
SP Championship Champions of the Court	C30	30.00
SP Championship Champions of the Court Die-Cut	C30D	225.00
SP Championship Championship Shots	S16	10.00
SP Championship Championship Shots Gold	S16	100.00
SP Championship Jordan Collection	JC17	12.00
SP Championship Jordan Collection	JC18	12.00
SP Championship Jordan Collection	JC19	12.00
SP Championship Jordan Collection	JC20	12.00
Stadium Club	1	5.00
Stadium Club Beam Team	BT14	50.00
Stadium Club Nemeses	N10	30.00
Stadium Club Reign Men	RM2	50.00
Stadium Club Spike Says	SS1	15.00
Stadium Club Warp Speed	WS1	60.00
Stadium Club Members Only 50	20	6.00
Stadium Club Members Only I	1	15.00
Stadium Club Members Only I	N10	40.00
Stadium Club Members Only I	WS1	40.00
Stadium Club Members Only II	B14	40.00
Stadium Club Members Only II	RM2	40.00
Stadium Club Members Only II	SS1	10.00
Topps	1	1.50
Topps	4	1.50
Topps	277	3.00
Topps Gallery	10	6.00
Topps Gallery Expressionists	EX2	50.00
Topps Mystery Finest	M1	50.00
Topps Mystery Finest Refractors	M1	300.00
Topps Power Boosters	1	80.00
Topps Power Boosters	4	60.00
Topps Power Boosters	277	50.00
Topps Show Stoppers	SS1	40.00
Topps Spark Plugs	SP2	15.00
Topps Top Flight	TF1	30.00
Topps World Class	WC1	25.00
Ultra	25	5.00
Ultra Gold Medallion	25	30.00
Ultra Double Trouble	3	8.00
Ultra Double Trouble Gold Medallion	3	25.00
Ultra Fabulous Fifties	5	15.00
Ultra Fabulous Fifties Gold Medallion	5	50.00
Ultra Jam City	3	30.00
Ultra Jam City Hot Pack	3	10.00
Ultra Scoring Kings	4	50.00
Ultra Scoring Kings Hot Pack	4	12.00

1995-1999 THE GOLDEN YEARS

Card	#	Price
Upper Deck	23	5.00
Upper Deck	137	2.50
Upper Deck	335	2.50
Upper Deck	337	1.25
Upper Deck	339	1.25
Upper Deck	341	1.25
Upper Deck	352	2.50
Upper Deck Ball Park Jordan	BP1	8.00
Upper Deck Ball Park Jordan	BP2	8.00
Upper Deck Ball Park Jordan	BP3	8.00
Upper Deck Ball Park Jordan	BP4	8.00
Upper Deck Ball Park Jordan	BP5	8.00
Upper Deck Ball Park Jordan Gold	1	12.00
Upper Deck Ball Park Jordan Gold	2	12.00
Upper Deck Ball Park Jordan Gold	3	12.00
Upper Deck Ball Park Jordan Gold	4	12.00
Upper Deck Ball Park Jordan Gold	5	12.00
Upper Deck Electric Court	23	12.00
Upper Deck Electric Court	137	6.00
Upper Deck Electric Court	335	6.00
Upper Deck Electric Court	337	3.00
Upper Deck Electric Court	339	3.00
Upper Deck Electric Court	341	3.00
Upper Deck Electric Court	352	6.00
Upper Deck Electric Court Gold	23	125.00
Upper Deck Electric Court Gold	137	60.00
Upper Deck Electric Court Gold	335	60.00
Upper Deck Electric Court Gold	337	30.00
Upper Deck Electric Court Gold	339	30.00
Upper Deck Electric Court Gold	341	30.00
Upper Deck Electric Court Gold	352	60.00
Upper Deck Jordan Collection	JC5	10.00
Upper Deck Jordan Collection	JC6	10.00
Upper Deck Jordan Collection	JC7	10.00
Upper Deck Jordan Collection	JC8	10.00
Upper Deck Jordan Collection	JC13	10.00
Upper Deck Jordan Collection	JC14	10.00
Upper Deck Jordan Collection	JC15	10.00
Upper Deck Jordan Collection	JC16	10.00
Upper Deck Predictor MVP	R1	8.00
Upper Deck Predictor MVP	R2	8.00
Upper Deck Predictor MVP	R3	8.00
Upper Deck Predictor MVP	R4	8.00
Upper Deck Predictor MVP	R5	8.00
Upper Deck Predictor MVP Redemption	R1	4.00
Upper Deck Predictor MVP Redemption	R2	4.00
Upper Deck Predictor MVP Redemption	R3	4.00
Upper Deck Predictor MVP Redemption	R4	4.00
Upper Deck Predictor MVP Redemption	R5	4.00
Upper Deck Predictor Player of the Month	R1	8.00
Upper Deck Predictor Player of the Month	R2	8.00
Upper Deck Predictor Player of the Month	R3	8.00
Upper Deck Predictor Player of the Month	R4	8.00
Upper Deck Predictor Player of the Month	R5	8.00
Upper Deck Predictor Player of the Month Redemption	R1	4.00
Upper Deck Predictor Player of the Month Redemption	R2	4.00
Upper Deck Predictor Player of the Month Redemption	R3	4.00
Upper Deck Predictor Player of the Month Redemption	R4	4.00
Upper Deck Predictor Player of the Month Redemption	R5	4.00
Upper Deck Predictor Player of the Week	H1	8.00
Upper Deck Predictor Player of the Week	H2	8.00
Upper Deck Predictor Player of the Week	H3	8.00
Upper Deck Predictor Player of the Week	H4	8.00
Upper Deck Predictor Player of the Week	H5	8.00
Upper Deck Predictor Player of the Week Redemption	H1	4.00
Upper Deck Predictor Player of the Week Redemption	H2	4.00
Upper Deck Predictor Player of the Week Redemption	H3	4.00
Upper Deck Predictor Player of the Week Redemption	H4	4.00
Upper Deck Predictor Player of the Week Redemption	H5	4.00
Upper Deck Predictor Scoring	H1	8.00
Upper Deck Predictor Scoring	H2	8.00
Upper Deck Predictor Scoring	H3	8.00

THE GOLDEN YEARS 1995-1999

Set	No.	Price
Upper Deck Predictor Scoring	H4	8.00
Upper Deck Predictor Scoring	H5	8.00
Upper Deck Predictor Scoring Redemption	H1	4.00
Upper Deck Predictor Scoring Redemption	H2	4.00
Upper Deck Predictor Scoring Redemption	H3	4.00
Upper Deck Predictor Scoring Redemption	H4	4.00
Upper Deck Predictor Scoring Redemption	H5	4.00
Upper Deck Special Edition	100	12.00
Upper Deck Special Edition Gold	100	100.00
Upper Deck Sheets	2	

1996-97

Set	No.	Price
Bowman's Best	80	8.00
Bowman's Best Atomic Refractors	80	250.00
Bowman's Best Refractors	80	100.00
Bowman's Best Cuts	BC2	40.00
Bowman's Best Cut Atomic Refractors	BC2	200.00
Bowman's Best Cut Refractors	BC2	100.00
Bowman's Best Honor Roll	HR2	60.00
Bowman's Best Honor Roll Atomic Refractors	HR2	350.00
Bowman's Best Honor Roll Refractors	HR2	175.00
Bowman's Best Shots	BS6	20.00
Bowman's Best Shot Atomic Refractors	BS6	80.00
Bowman's Best Shot Refractors	BS6	40.00
Collector's Choice	23	2.50
Collector's Choice	25	1.25
Collector's Choice	26	1.25
Collector's Choice	195	1.25
Collector's Choice	196	.15
Collector's Choice	356	1.25
Collector's Choice	362	.75
Collector's Choice	363	.75
Collector's Choice	364	.75
Collector's Choice	365	1.00
Collector's Choice	366	1.00
Collector's Choice	370	1.25
Collector's Choice	F1	4.00
Collector's Choice	NNO	5.00
Collector's Choice	NNO	5.00
Collector's Choice Chicago Bulls Team Set	B1	2.00
Collector's Choice Chicago Bulls Team Set	CH3	3.00
Collector's Choice Crash the Game Scoring 1	C30A	12.00
Collector's Choice Crash the Game Scoring 1	C30B	12.00
Collector's Choice Crash the Game Scoring 1 Redemption	R30	15.00
Collector's Choice Crash the Game Scoring Gold 1	C30A	75.00
Collector's Choice Crash the Game Scoring Gold 1	C30B	75.00
Collector's Choice Crash the Game Scoring Gold 1 Redemption	R30	75.00
Collector's Choice Crash the Game Scoring 2	C30A	15.00
Collector's Choice Crash the Game Scoring 2	C30B	15.00
Collector's Choice Crash the Game Scoring 2 Redemption	R30	15.00
Collector's Choice Crash the Game Scoring Gold 2	C30A	75.00
Collector's Choice Crash the Game Scoring Gold 2	C30B	75.00
Collector's Choice Crash the Game Scoring Gold 2 Redemption	R30	75.00
Collector's Choice Factory Blow-Ups	1	4.00
Collector's Choice Factory Blow-Ups	4	4.00
Collector's Choice Game Face	GF2	8.00
Collector's Choice Jordan A Cut Above	CA1	2.50
Collector's Choice Jordan A Cut Above	CA2	2.50
Collector's Choice Jordan A Cut Above	CA3	2.50
Collector's Choice Jordan A Cut Above	CA4	2.50
Collector's Choice Jordan A Cut Above	CA5	2.50
Collector's Choice Jordan A Cut Above	CA6	2.50
Collector's Choice Jordan A Cut Above	CA7	2.50
Collector's Choice Jordan A Cut Above	CA8	2.50
Collector's Choice Jordan A Cut Above	CA9	2.50
Collector's Choice Jordan A Cut Above	CA10	2.50
Collector's Choice Int'l I	20	3.00
Collector's Choice Int'l I	169	1.50
Collector's Choice Int'l I	173	2.00
Collector's Choice Int'l I	195	1.50

1995-1999 THE GOLDEN YEARS

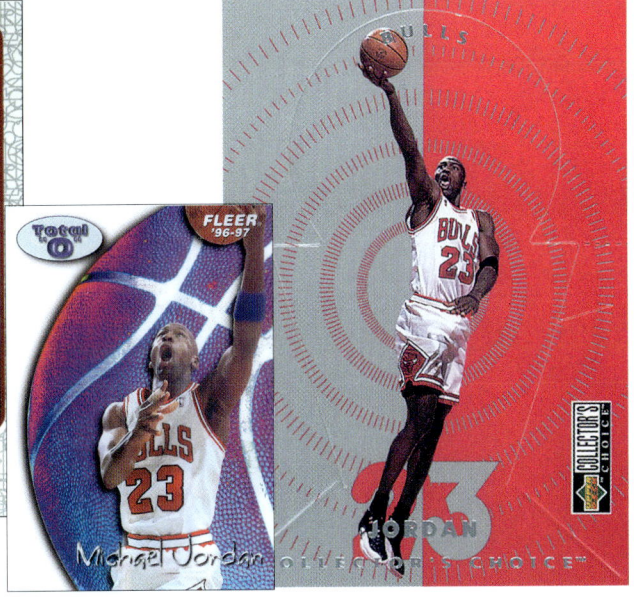

Set	Card #	Price
Collector's Choice Int'l I	210	.75
Collector's Choice Int'l II	114	1.50
Collector's Choice Int'l II	143	1.50
Collector's Choice Int'l II	200	.75
Collector's Choice Int'l Japanese	45	10.00
Collector's Choice Int'l Japanese	169	5.00
Collector's Choice Int'l Japanese	173	4.50
Collector's Choice Int'l Japanese	195	5.00
Collector's Choice Int'l Japanese	210	2.50
Collector's Choice Int'l Japanese	324	5.00
Collector's Choice Int'l Japanese	353	5.00
Collector's Choice Int'l Japanese	410	2.50
Collector's Choice Int'l Jordan Collection	JC1	4.00
Collector's Choice Int'l Jordan Collection	JC2	4.00
Collector's Choice Int'l Jordan Collection	JC3	4.00
Collector's Choice Int'l Jordan Collection	JC4	4.00
Collector's Choice Memorable Moments	1	8.00
Collector's Choice Mini-Cards	M78	5.00
Collector's Choice Mini-Cards Gold	M78	60.00
Collector's Choice Stick-Ums 1	S30	4.00
Collector's Choice Stick-Ums 2	S30	4.00
Finest	50	10.00
Finest	127	30.00
Finest	291	125.00
Finest Refractors	50	150.00
Finest Refractors	127	200.00
Finest Refractors	291	800.00
Flair Showcase Row 2	23	10.00
Flair Showcase Row 1	23	15.00
Flair Showcase Row 0	23	125.00
Flair Showcase Legacy Collection - Row 2	23	600.00
Flair Showcase Legacy Collection - Row 1	23	600.00
Flair Showcase Legacy Collection - Row 0	23	600.00
Flair Showcase Hot Shots	1	175.00
Fleer	13	3.00
Fleer	123	1.50
Fleer	282	1.50
Fleer Decade of Excellence	4	80.00
Fleer European	13	
Fleer European	123	
Fleer European	312	
Fleer Game Breakers	1	100.00
Fleer Stackhouse's All-Fleer	4	10.00
Fleer Thrill Seekers	6	200.00
Fleer Total O	4	60.00
Hoops	20	3.00
Hoops	176	1.50
Hoops	335	1.50
Hoops Silver	20	10.00
Hoops Head to Head	HH2	20.00
Hoops Hot List	8	50.00
Hoops Starting Five	4	12.00
Hoops Superfeats	1	60.00
Metal	11	5.00
Metal	128	2.50
Metal	241	2.50
Metal Precious Metal	241	250.00
Metal Decade of Excellence	M4	40.00
Metal Maximum Metal	4	125.00
Metal Molten Metal	18	100.00
Metal Net-Rageous	5	175.00
Metal Platinum Portraits	5	60.00
Metal Steel Slammin'	6	80.00
SkyBox	16	4.00
SkyBox	247	2.00
SkyBox Rubies	16	150.00
SkyBox Rubies	247	80.00
SkyBox Golden Touch	5	150.00
SkyBox Larger Than Life	B7	175.00
SkyBox Net Set	8	60.00
SkyBox Thunder and Lightning	1	80.00
SkyBox Triple Threats	TT11	80.00
SkyBox E-X2000	9	15.00
SkyBox E-X2000 Credentials	9	350.00
SkyBox E-X2000 A Cut Above	5	200.00
SkyBox E-X2000 Net Assets	8	60.00
SkyBox Z-Force	11	5.00
SkyBox Z-Force	179	2.00
SkyBox Z-Force Z-Cling	11	12.00
SkyBox Z-Force Big Men on the Court	4	175.00
SkyBox Z-Force Big Men on the Court Z-peat	4	350.00
SkyBox Z-Force Slam Cam	SC5	150.00

THE GOLDEN YEARS 1995-1999

Card	#	Price
SkyBox Z-Force Vortex	V5	50.00
SP	16	5.00
SP Game Film	GF1	125.00
SP Holoviews	PC5	40.00
SP Inside Info	IN17	60.00
SP Inside Info Gold	IN17	200.00
SP SPx Force	F1	100.00
SP SPx Force	F5	110.00
SP SPx Force	F5A	2500.00
SPx	8	20.00
SPx	R1	20.00
SPx Autograph	NNO	3000.00
SPx Expired Exchange	NNO	500.00
SPx Gold	8	40.00
SPx Holoview Heroes	H1	30.00
Stadium Club	101	5.00
Stadium Club Class Acts	CA1	20.00
Stadium Club Class Acts Atomic Refractors	CA1	120.00
Stadium Club Class Acts Refractors	CA1	60.00
Stadium Club Finest Reprints	24	40.00
Stadium Club Finest Reprint Refractors	24	120.00
Stadium Club Fusion	F1	50.00
Stadium Club Gallery Player's Private Issue	10	250.00
Stadium Club Golden Moments	GM3	4.00
Stadium Club High Risers	HR14	50.00
Stadium Club Shining Moments	SM2	5.00
Stadium Club Special Forces	SF4	25.00
Stadium Club Top Crop	TC9	30.00
Stadium Club Members Only 55	41	5.00
Stadium Club Members Only I	F1	20.00
Stadium Club Members Only I	GM3	2.00
Stadium Club Members Only I	SF4	12.00
Stadium Club Members Only I	SM2	2.50
Stadium Club Members Only I	TC9	12.00
Stadium Club Members Only II	101	20.00
Stadium Club Members Only II	CA1	12.00
Stadium Club Members Only II	HR14	20.00
Topps	139	3.00
Topps NBA at 50	139	20.00
Topps Holding Court	HC2	40.00
Topps Holding Court Refractors	HC2	80.00
Topps Chrome	139	40.00
Topps Chrome Refractors	139	400.00
Topps Chrome Pro Files	PF3	15.00
Topps Chrome Season's Best	SB1	15.00
Topps Chrome Season's Best	SB18	15.00
Topps Mystery Finest	M14	50.00
Topps Mystery Finest Bordered Refractors	M14	300.00
Topps Mystery Finest Borderless	M14	75.00
Topps Mystery Finest Borderless Refractors	M14	300.00
Topps Pro Files	PF3	10.00
Topps Season's Best	SB1	15.00
Topps Season's Best	SB18	15.00
Topps Stars	24	3.00
Topps Stars	74	3.00
Topps Stars	124	3.00
Topps Stars Finest	24	35.00
Topps Stars Finest	74	35.00
Topps Stars Finest	124	35.00
Topps Stars Finest Atomic Refractors	24	400.00
Topps Stars Finest Atomic Refractors	74	400.00
Topps Stars Finest Atomic Refractors	124	400.00
Topps Stars Finest Refractors	24	200.00
Topps Stars Finest Refractors	74	200.00
Topps Stars Finest Refractors	124	200.00
Topps Stars Imagine	I6	40.00
Topps Stars Reprints	24	50.00
Topps Super Teams	ST4	150.00
Topps Super Teams Conference Winners	M14	20.00
Topps Super Teams Division Winners	M14	10.00
Topps Super Teams NBA Finals	M14	50.00
Ultra	16	5.00
Ultra	143	2.50
Ultra	280	2.50
Ultra Gold Edition	G16	60.00
Ultra Gold Edition	G143	30.00
Ultra Gold Edition	G280	30.00
Ultra Platinum Edition	P16	400.00
Ultra Platinum Edition	P143	200.00
Ultra Platinum Edition	P280	200.00
Ultra Board Game	7	20.00
Ultra Court Masters	2	150.00

1995-1999 THE GOLDEN YEARS

Ultra Decade of Excellence	U4	40.00
Ultra Full Court Trap	1	20.00
Ultra Full Court Trap Gold	1	125.00
Ultra Give and Take	5	30.00
Ultra Scoring Kings	4	60.00
Ultra Scoring Kings Plus	4	150.00
Ultra Starring Role	4	150.00
Upper Deck	16	5.00
Upper Deck	139	2.00
Upper Deck	165	2.50
Upper Deck Ball Park Jordan	1	8.00
Upper Deck Ball Park Jordan	2	8.00
Upper Deck Ball Park Jordan	3	8.00
Upper Deck Ball Park Jordan	4	8.00
Upper Deck Ball Park Jordan	5	8.00
Upper Deck Ball Park Jordan Gold	1	6.00
Upper Deck Ball Park Jordan Gold	2	6.00
Upper Deck Ball Park Jordan Gold	3	6.00
Upper Deck Ball Park Jordan Gold	4	6.00
Upper Deck Ball Park Jordan Gold	5	6.00
Upper Deck Fast Break Connections	FB23	30.00
Upper Deck Jordan Greater Heights	GH1	25.00
Upper Deck Jordan Greater Heights	GH2	25.00
Upper Deck Jordan Greater Heights	GH3	25.00
Upper Deck Jordan Greater Heights	GH4	25.00
Upper Deck Jordan Greater Heights	GH5	25.00
Upper Deck Jordan Greater Heights	GH6	25.00
Upper Deck Jordan Greater Heights	GH7	25.00
Upper Deck Jordan Greater Heights	GH8	25.00
Upper Deck Jordan Greater Heights	GH9	25.00
Upper Deck Jordan Greater Heights	GH10	25.00
Upper Deck Jordan's Viewpoints	VP1	15.00
Upper Deck Jordan's Viewpoints	VP2	15.00
Upper Deck Jordan's Viewpoints	VP3	15.00
Upper Deck Jordan's Viewpoints	VP4	15.00
Upper Deck Jordan's Viewpoints	VP5	15.00
Upper Deck Jordan's Viewpoints	VP6	15.00
Upper Deck Jordan's Viewpoints	VP7	15.00
Upper Deck Jordan's Viewpoints	VP8	15.00
Upper Deck Jordan's Viewpoints	VP9	15.00
Upper Deck Jordan's Viewpoints	VP10	15.00
Upper Deck Michael's Viewpoints Jumbos	VP1	1.00
Upper Deck Michael's Viewpoints Jumbos	VP2	1.00
Upper Deck Michael's Viewpoints Jumbos	VP3	1.00
Upper Deck Michael's Viewpoints Jumbos	VP4	1.00
Upper Deck Michael's Viewpoints Jumbos	VP5	1.00
Upper Deck Michael's Viewpoints Jumbos	VP6	1.00
Upper Deck Michael's Viewpoints Jumbos	VP7	1.00
Upper Deck Michael's Viewpoints Jumbos	VP8	1.00
Upper Deck Michael's Viewpoints Jumbos	VP9	1.00
Upper Deck Michael's Viewpoints Jumbos	VP10	1.00
Upper Deck Nestle Slam Dunk	4	
Upper Deck Predictor Scoring 1	P3	25.00
Upper Deck Predictor TV Cel Redemption 1	TV3	50.00
Upper Deck Predictor Scoring 2	P2	25.00
Upper Deck Predictor TV Cel Redemption 2	TV2	50.00
Upper Deck Rookie of the Year Collection	RC13	100.00
Upper Deck Smooth Grooves	SG8	80.00
Upper Deck 23 Nights Jordan Experience	1	1.50
Upper Deck 23 Nights Jordan Experience	2	1.50
Upper Deck 23 Nights Jordan Experience	3	1.50
Upper Deck 23 Nights Jordan Experience	4	1.50
Upper Deck 23 Nights Jordan Experience	5	1.50
Upper Deck 23 Nights Jordan Experience	6	1.50
Upper Deck 23 Nights Jordan Experience	7	1.50
Upper Deck 23 Nights Jordan Experience	8	1.50
Upper Deck 23 Nights Jordan Experience	9	1.50
Upper Deck 23 Nights Jordan Experience	10	1.50
Upper Deck 23 Nights Jordan Experience	11	1.50
Upper Deck 23 Nights Jordan Experience	12	1.50
Upper Deck 23 Nights Jordan Experience	13	1.50
Upper Deck 23 Nights Jordan Experience	14	1.50
Upper Deck 23 Nights Jordan Experience	15	1.50
Upper Deck 23 Nights Jordan Experience	16	1.50
Upper Deck 23 Nights Jordan Experience	17	1.50
Upper Deck 23 Nights Jordan Experience	18	1.50
Upper Deck 23 Nights Jordan Experience	19	1.50
Upper Deck 23 Nights Jordan Experience	20	1.50
Upper Deck 23 Nights Jordan Experience	21	1.50
Upper Deck 23 Nights Jordan Experience	22	1.50
Upper Deck 23 Nights Jordan Experience	23	1.50
Upper Deck 23 Nights Jordan Experience	NNO	1.00

MICHAEL JORDAN COLLECTIBLES

THE GOLDEN YEARS 1995-1999

Set	No.	Price
Upper Deck 23 Nights Jordan Experience	NNO	5.00
Upper Deck UD3	23	10.00
Upper Deck UD3 Court Commemorative Autograph Exchange	C1	2500.00
Upper Deck UD3 Superstar Spotlight	S5	100.00
Upper Deck UD3 The Winning Edge	W1	30.00
Upper Deck USA Michael Jordan American Made	M1	25.00
Upper Deck USA Michael Jordan American Made	M2	25.00
Upper Deck USA Michael Jordan American Made	M3	25.00
Upper Deck USA Michael Jordan American Made	M4	25.00
Upper Deck U.S. Olympic Champions	11	3.00
Upper Deck U.S. Olympic Champions	134	1.50
Upper Deck U.S. Olympic Champions Reflections of Gold	RG1	12.00
Upper Deck U.S. Olympic Champions Reflections of Gold Signatures	RG1	4000.00
Upper Deck U.S. Olympic Champions Reign of Gold Holograms	RN1	15.00
Upper Deck Italian Stickers	88	2.50
Upper Deck Italian Stickers	89	2.50
Upper Deck Italian Stickers	90	2.50
Upper Deck Italian Stickers	91	2.50
Upper Deck Italian Stickers	114	5.00

1997-98

Set	No.	Price
Bleachers/Fleer Gold	6	
Bleachers/Fleer Gold Black Foil	6	
Bleachers/Fleer Gold Holographic Foil	6	
Bowman's Best	60	6.00
Bowman's Best	96	3.00
Bowman's Best Atomic Refractors	60	150.00
Bowman's Best Atomic Refractors	96	80.00
Bowman's Best Refractors	60	75.00
Bowman's Best Refractors	96	40.00
Bowman's Best Mirror Image	MI1	50.00
Bowman's Best Mirror Image Atomic Refractors	MI1	150.00
Bowman's Best Mirror Image Refractors	MI1	75.00
Bowman's Best Techniques	T2	20.00
Bowman's Best Technique Atomic Refractor	T2	100.00
Bowman's Best Technique Refractors	T2	50.00
Collector's Choice	23	2.50
Collector's Choice	159	1.25
Collector's Choice	185	1.25
Collector's Choice	186	1.00
Collector's Choice	187	1.00
Collector's Choice	188	1.00
Collector's Choice	189	1.00
Collector's Choice	190	1.00
Collector's Choice	191	1.00
Collector's Choice	192	1.00
Collector's Choice	193	1.00
Collector's Choice	194	1.00
Collector's Choice	195	1.00
Collector's Choice	385	1.00
Collector's Choice	386	1.00
Collector's Choice	387	1.00
Collector's Choice	388	1.00
Collector's Choice	389	1.00
Collector's Choice	390	1.00
Collector's Choice	391	1.00
Collector's Choice	392	1.00
Collector's Choice	393	1.00
Collector's Choice	394	1.00
Collector's Choice	395	1.00
Collector's Choice Crash the Game Scoring	C30A	15.00
Collector's Choice Crash the Game Scoring	C30B	15.00
Collector's Choice Crash the Game Scoring Redemption	R30	8.00
Collector's Choice Int'l Italian 1	23	8.00
Collector's Choice Int'l Italian 1	25	4.00
Collector's Choice Int'l Italian 1	26	4.00
Collector's Choice Int'l Italian 1	195	4.00
Collector's Choice Int'l Italian Crash the Game Scoring	C30A	30.00

1995-1999 THE GOLDEN YEARS

Collector's Choice Int'l Italian Crash the Game Scoring	C30B	30.00
Collector's Choice Int'l Italian Jordan's Journal	J1	10.00
Collector's Choice Int'l Italian Jordan's Journal	J2	10.00
Collector's Choice Int'l Italian Jordan's Journal	J3	10.00
Collector's Choice Int'l Italian Jordan's Journal	J4	10.00
Collector's Choice Int'l Italian Jordan's Journal	J5	10.00
Collector's Choice Int'l Italian Jordan's Journal	J6	10.00
Collector's Choice Int'l Italian Mini-Cards	M78	10.00
Collector's Choice Int'l Italian Stick Ums	S30	10.00
Collector's Choice Miniatures	M30	3.00
Collector's Choice MJ Bullseye	B1	6.00
Collector's Choice MJ Bullseye	B2	6.00
Collector's Choice MJ Bullseye	B3	4.00
Collector's Choice MJ Bullseye	B4	4.00
Collector's Choice MJ Bullseye	B5	4.00
Collector's Choice MJ Bullseye	B6	6.00
Collector's Choice MJ Bullseye	B7	6.00
Collector's Choice MJ Bullseye	B8	4.00
Collector's Choice MJ Bullseye	B9	6.00
Collector's Choice MJ Bullseye	B10	6.00
Collector's Choice MJ Bullseye	B11	4.00
Collector's Choice MJ Bullseye	B12	4.00
Collector's Choice MJ Bullseye	B13	6.00
Collector's Choice MJ Bullseye	B14	6.00
Collector's Choice MJ Bullseye	B15	6.00
Collector's Choice MJ Bullseye	B16	6.00
Collector's Choice MJ Bullseye	B17	6.00
Collector's Choice MJ Bullseye	B18	6.00
Collector's Choice MJ Bullseye	B19	6.00
Collector's Choice MJ Bullseye	B20	4.00
Collector's Choice MJ Bullseye	B21	6.00
Collector's Choice MJ Bullseye	B22	4.00
Collector's Choice MJ Bullseye	B23	6.00
Collector's Choice MJ Bullseye	B24	6.00
Collector's Choice MJ Bullseye	B25	4.00
Collector's Choice MJ Bullseye	B26	6.00
Collector's Choice MJ Bullseye	B27	6.00
Collector's Choice MJ Bullseye	B28	6.00
Collector's Choice MJ Bullseye	B29	6.00
Collector's Choice MJ Bullseye	B30	6.00
Collector's Choice MJ Rewind Redemption	R1	4.00
Collector's Choice MJ Rewind Redemption	R2	4.00
Collector's Choice MJ Rewind Redemption	R3	4.00
Collector's Choice MJ Rewind Redemption	R4	4.00
Collector's Choice MJ Rewind Redemption	R5	4.00
Collector's Choice MJ Rewind Redemption	R6	4.00
Collector's Choice MJ Rewind Redemption	R7	4.00
Collector's Choice MJ Rewind Redemption	R8	4.00
Collector's Choice MJ Rewind Redemption	R9	4.00
Collector's Choice MJ Rewind Redemption	R10	4.00
Collector's Choice MJ Rewind Redemption	R11	4.00
Collector's Choice MJ Rewind Redemption	R12	4.00
Collector's Choice MJ Rewind Redemption	R13	4.00
Collector's Choice Star Attractions	SA1	10.00
Collector's Choice Star Attractions Gold	SA1	50.00
Collector's Choice StarQuest	83	80.00
Collector's Choice StarQuest	171	80.00
Collector's Choice Stick-Ums	S30	3.00
Collector's Choice The Jordan Dynasty	1	15.00
Collector's Choice The Jordan Dynasty	2	15.00
Collector's Choice The Jordan Dynasty	3	15.00
Collector's Choice The Jordan Dynasty	4	15.00
Collector's Choice The Jordan Dynasty	5	15.00
Collector's Choice Catch 23	C1	
Collector's Choice Catch 23	C2	
Collector's Choice Catch 23	C3	
Collector's Choice Catch 23	C4	
Collector's Choice Catch 23	C5	
Collector's Choice Catch 23	C6	
Collector's Choice Catch 23	C7	
Collector's Choice Catch 23	C8	
Collector's Choice Catch 23	C9	
Collector's Choice Catch 23	C10	
Collector's Choice Jumbos	1	
Collector's Choice Jumbos	2	

MICHAEL JORDAN COLLECTIBLES 67

THE GOLDEN YEARS 1995-1999

Card	#	Value
Collector's Choice Jumbos	3	
Collector's Choice Jumbos	4	
Collector's Choice Jumbos	5	
Collector's Choice Jumbos	6	
Collector's Choice Jumbos	7	
Collector's Choice Jumbos	8	
Collector's Choice Jumbos	9	
Collector's Choice Jumbos	10	
Finest	39	6.00
Finest	154	80.00
Finest	271	6.00
Finest	287	25.00
Finest Embossed	154	120.00
Finest Embossed	287	40.00
Finest Embossed Refractors	154	1,800.00
Finest Embossed Refractors	287	400.00
Finest Refractors	39	80.00
Finest Refractors	154	500.00
Finest Refractors	271	80.00
Finest Refractors	287	100.00
Flair Showcase Row 3	1	10.00
Flair Showcase Row 2	1	20.00
Flair Showcase Row 1	1	50.00
Flair Showcase Row 0	1	300.00
Flair Showcase Legacy Collection - Row 3	1	700.00
Flair Showcase Legacy Collection - Row 2	1	700.00
Flair Showcase Legacy Collection - Row 1	1	700.00
Flair Showcase Legacy Collection - Row 0	1	700.00
Flair Showcase Masterpiece - Row 3	1	
Flair Showcase Masterpiece - Row 2	1	
Flair Showcase Masterpiece - Row 1	1	
Flair Showcase Masterpiece - Row 0	1	
Fleer	23	3.00
Fleer Crystal Collection	23	15.00
Fleer Tiffany Collection	23	100.00
Fleer Decade of Excellence	5	60.00
Fleer Decade of Excellence Rare Traditions	5	250.00
Fleer Flair Hardwood Leaders	4	15.00
Fleer Game Breakers	1	150.00
Fleer Soaring Stars	9	5.00
Fleer High Flying Soaring Stars	9	20.00
Fleer Thrill Seekers	7	100.00
Fleer Total O	5	20.00
Fleer Zone	10	40.00
Hoops	1	1.50
Hoops	220	3.00
Hoops Dish N Swish	DS5	30.00
Hoops Frequent Flyer Club	FF4	30.00
Hoops Frequent Flyer Club Upgrade	FF4	125.00
Hoops High Voltage	HV14	30.00
Hoops High Voltage 500	HV14	150.00
Hoops HOOPerstars	H1	120.00
Hoops 911	N1	120.00
Hoops Rock the House	RH6	30.00
Metal Universe	23	5.00
Metal Universe Precious Metal Gems Red	23	750.00
Metal Universe Precious Metal Gems Green	23	8,500.00
Metal Universe Planet Metal	1	30.00
Metal Universe Platinum Portraits	1	150.00
Metal Universe Titanium	1	80.00
Metal Universe Championship	23	5.00
Metal Universe Championship Precious Metal Gems	23	1,200.00
Metal Universe Championship All-Millenium Team	5	10.00
Metal Universe Championship Championship Galaxy	1	100.00
Metal Universe Championship Hardware	5	200.00
SkyBox	29	5.00
SkyBox	235	10.00
SkyBox Star Rubies	29	2,000.00
SkyBox Star Rubies	235	1,600.00
SkyBox And One	10	60.00
SkyBox Competitive Advantage	CA3	60.00
SkyBox Golden Touch	GT1	200.00
SkyBox Premium Players	1	110.00
SkyBox Silky Smooth	1	200.00
SkyBox Thunder and Lightning	TL5	100.00
SkyBox E-X2001	9	15.00
SkyBox E-X2001 Essential Credentials Future	9	1,200.00
SkyBox E-X2001 Essential Credentials Now	9	
SkyBox E-X2001 Gravity Denied	9	50.00

68 EVERYTHING YOU NEED TO KNOW ABOUT

1995-1999 THE GOLDEN YEARS

SkyBox E-X2001 Jam-Balaya	6	350.00
SkyBox Z-Force	23	3.00
SkyBox Z-Force	190	1.50
SkyBox Z-Force Rave	23	200.00
SkyBox Z-Force Rave	190	100.00
SkyBox Z-Force Super Rave	190	1,600.00
SkyBox Z-Force Big Men on Court	9	150.00
SkyBox Z-Force Boss	10	10.00
SkyBox Z-Force Super Boss	10	30.00
SkyBox Z-Force Limited Access	6	25.00
SkyBox Z-Force Quick Strike	5	50.00
SkyBox Z-Force Rave Reviews	6	120.00
SkyBox Z-Force Slam Cam	5	30.00
SP Authentic	23	8.00
SP Authentic Authentics - AU Jersey	MJ1	2,500.00
SP Authentic Authentics - AU 16X20	MJ2	600.00
SP Authentic Authentics - 2-card set	MJ3	60.00
SP Authentic Authentics - 8x10	MJ4	60.00
SP Authentic Authentics - Gold card	MJ5	100.00
SP Authentic Authentics - Game Night card #'d to 100	MJ6	500.00
SP Authentic Authentics - Game Night card #'d to 100	MJ6B	500.00
SP Authentic Authentics - Game Night card #'d to 100	MJ6C	500.00
SP Authentic Authentics - Game Night card #'d to 100	MJ6D	500.00
SP Authentic Authentics - Game Night card #'d to 100	MJ6E	500.00
SP Authentic Authentics - Poster	MJ7	80.00
SP Authentic Authentics - AU Game Night card	MJ8	7,000.00
SP Authentic BuyBack	21	3,000.00
SP Authentic Profiles 1	P1	12.00
SP Authentic Profiles 2	P1	30.00
SP Authentic Profiles 3	P1	700.00
SP Authentic Sign of the Times Stars and Rookies	MJ	
SPx	6	12.00
SPx Bronze	6	25.00
SPx Gold	6	100.00
SPx Silver	6	50.00
SPx Grand Finale	6	1,200.00
SPx Sky	6	15.00
SPx	5	20.00
SPx Promo	NNO	15.00
SPx Gold	5	40.00
SPx Hardcourt Holoview	HH1	80.00
SPx Holoview Heroes	H1	80.00
SPx ProMotion	1	120.00
SPx ProMotion Autographs	1	2,500.00
SPx ProMotion	PM1	150.00
Stadium Club	118	5.00
Stadium Club First Day Issue	118	150.00
Stadium Club Hardcourt Heroics	H1	15.00
Stadium Club Hoop Screams	HS10	15.00
Stadium Club Members Only I	H1	
Stadium Club Members Only I	T1B	
Stadium Club Members Only I	HS10	
Stadium Club Members Only II	118	
Stadium Club Members Only II	T9B	
Stadium Club Members Only II	NC1	
Stadium Club Members Only II	RC6	
Stadium Club Never Compromise	NC1	40.00
Stadium Club One Of A Kind	5	250.00
Stadium Club One Of A Kind	118	350.00
Stadium Club Printing Plates - Black	5	
Stadium Club Printing Plates - Cyan	5	
Stadium Club Printing Plates - Magenta	5	
Stadium Club Printing Plates - Yellow	5	
Stadium Club Printing Plates - Black	118	
Stadium Club Printing Plates - Cyan	118	
Stadium Club Printing Plates - Magenta	118	
Stadium Club Printing Plates - Yellow	118	
Stadium Club Royal Court	RC6	20.00
Stadium Club Triumvirate	T1B	60.00
Stadium Club Triumvirate	T9B	60.00
Stadium Club Triumvirate Illuminator	T1B	300.00
Stadium Club Triumvirate Illuminator	T9B	300.00
Stadium Club Triumvirate Luminescent	T1B	180.00
Stadium Club Triumvirate Luminescent	T9B	180.00
Topps	123	3.00

THE GOLDEN YEARS 1995-1999

Topps Bound for Glory	BG10	30.00
Topps Clutch Time	CT1	30.00
Topps Generations	G2	50.00
Topps Generation Refractors	G2	150.00
Topps Inside Stuff	IS1	20.00
Topps Minted in Springfield	123	15.00
Topps Rock Stars	RS1	40.00
Topps Rock Star Refractors	RS1	120.00
Topps Season's Best	SB6	20.00
Topps Topps 40	T5	20.00
Topps Chrome	123	20.00
Topps Chrome Refractors	123	350.00
Topps Chrome Season's Best	SB6	20.00
Topps Chrome Season's Best Refractors	SB6	60.00
Topps Chrome Topps 40	T5	20.00
Topps Chrome Topps 40 Refractors	T5	60.00
Ultra	23	5.00
Ultra	259	10.00
Ultra Gold Medallion	23	12.00
Ultra Gold Medallion	259	12.00
Ultra Masterpieces	23	
Ultra Masterpieces	259	
Ultra Platinum Medallion	23	750.00
Ultra Platinum Medallion	259	600.00
Ultra Big Shots	1	8.00
Ultra Court Masters	CM1	100.00
Ultra Star Power	SP1	8.00
Ultra Star Power Plus	SPP1	40.00
Ultra Star Power Supreme	SPS1	250.00
Ultra Stars	1	100.00
Ultra Stars Gold	1	400.00
Ultra Ultrabilities	1	8.00
Ultra Ultrabilities All-Star	1	40.00
Ultra Ultrabilities Superstar	1	250.00
Ultra View to a Thrill	VT1	20.00
Upper Deck	18	5.00
Upper Deck	139	2.50
Upper Deck	165	2.50
Upper Deck	316	2.50
Upper Deck	334	1.00
Upper Deck - Red Audio	NNO	12.00
Upper Deck - Black Audio	NNO	30.00
Upper Deck - White Audio	NNO	
Upper Deck AIRlines	AL1	100.00
Upper Deck AIRlines	AL2	100.00
Upper Deck AIRlines	AL3	100.00
Upper Deck AIRlines	AL4	100.00
Upper Deck AIRlines	AL5	100.00
Upper Deck AIRlines	AL6	100.00
Upper Deck AIRlines	AL7	100.00
Upper Deck AIRlines	AL8	100.00
Upper Deck AIRlines	AL9	100.00
Upper Deck AIRlines	AL10	100.00
Upper Deck AIRlines	AL11	100.00
Upper Deck AIRlines	AL12	100.00
Upper Deck Championship Journals	1	1.50
Upper Deck Championship Journals	2	1.50
Upper Deck Championship Journals	3	1.50
Upper Deck Championship Journals	4	1.50
Upper Deck Championship Journals	5	1.50
Upper Deck Championship Journals	6	1.50
Upper Deck Championship Journals	7	1.50
Upper Deck Championship Journals	8	1.50
Upper Deck Championship Journals	9	1.50
Upper Deck Championship Journals	10	1.50
Upper Deck Championship Journals	11	1.50
Upper Deck Championship Journals	12	1.50
Upper Deck Championship Journals	13	1.50

1995-1999 THE GOLDEN YEARS

Set	No.	Price
Upper Deck Championship Journals	14	1.50
Upper Deck Championship Journals	15	1.50
Upper Deck Championship Journals	16	1.50
Upper Deck Championship Journals	17	1.50
Upper Deck Championship Journals	18	1.50
Upper Deck Championship Journals	19	1.50
Upper Deck Championship Journals	20	1.50
Upper Deck Championship Journals	21	1.50
Upper Deck Championship Journals	22	1.50
Upper Deck Championship Journals	23	1.50
Upper Deck Championship Journals	24	1.50
Upper Deck Championship Journals	NNO	5.00
Upper Deck Championship Journals	NNO	1500.00
Upper Deck Diamond Dimensions	D23	750.00
Upper Deck Diamond Vision	4	30.00
Upper Deck Diamond Vision Signature Moves	4	60.00
Upper Deck Diamond Vision Dunk Vision	D1	125.00
Upper Deck Diamond Vision Reel Time	R1	250.00
Upper Deck Game Dated Memorable Moments	18	800.00
Upper Deck Game Jerseys	GJ13	2,500.00
Upper Deck Game Jerseys	GJ13S	10,000.00
Upper Deck Great Eight	G5	200.00
Upper Deck Highlight Reels	1	15.00
Upper Deck Highlight Reels	2	15.00
Upper Deck Highlight Reels	3	15.00
Upper Deck Highlight Reels	4	15.00
Upper Deck Highlight Reels	5	15.00
Upper Deck High Dimensions	D23	100.00
Upper Deck Holojams	1	25.00
Upper Deck Jordan Air Time	AT1	10.00
Upper Deck Jordan Air Time	AT2	10.00
Upper Deck Jordan Air Time	AT3	10.00
Upper Deck Jordan Air Time	AT4	10.00
Upper Deck Jordan Air Time	AT5	10.00
Upper Deck Jordan Air Time	AT6	10.00
Upper Deck Jordan Air Time	AT7	10.00
Upper Deck Jordan Air Time	AT8	10.00
Upper Deck Jordan Air Time	AT9	10.00
Upper Deck Jordan Air Time	AT10	50.00
Upper Deck Nestle Crunch Time	CT5	
Upper Deck Nestle Slam Dunk	22	
Upper Deck Records Collection	RC30	40.00
Upper Deck Teammates	T7	12.00
Upper Deck Teammates	T59	12.00
Upper Deck Ultimates	U1	40.00
Upper Deck UD3	15	5.00
Upper Deck UD3	23	5.00
Upper Deck UD3	45	8.00
Upper Deck UD3 Awesome Action	A1	50.00
Upper Deck UD3 MJ3	MJ3-1	15.00
Upper Deck UD3 MJ3	MJ3-2	20.00
Upper Deck UD3 MJ3	MJ3-3	30.00
Upper Deck UD3 Season Ticket Autographs	MJ	2,500.00

1998-99

Set	No.	Price
Topps	77	3.00
Topps Apparitions	A15	30.00
Topps Roundball Royalty	R1	40.00
Topps Roundball Royalty Refractors	R1	100.00
Topps Season's Best	SB6	20.00
Upper Deck UD Choice Preview	23	2.00

1994-1995 BASEBALL YEARS

Michael's shocking NBA "retirement"
produced the unthinkable:
a sizzling lineup of baseball cards

MINOR SENSATION

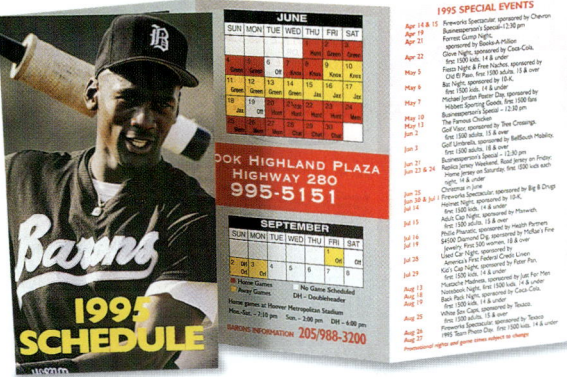

It was early fall, down time for most NBA stars, and yet here Michael Jordan was, playing professional sports. When the NBA's most recognizable player unexpectedly left basketball in 1994 to give baseball a try, the White Sox jumped at the opportunity, and Jordan eventually became the most recognizable player in the Arizona Fall League.

Michael drew record crowds whenever he played for the Scottsdale Scorpions. Fans cheered wildly whether he was getting a hit or getting picked off first base. His bat was weak. His defense rather frightening. But Jordan helped keep the league alive because of the enormous revenue he generated. Scottsdale drew 1,673 fans per game — more than twice the league average — while boosting road game attendance as well.

After breaking into professional baseball with Double-A Birmingham in the summer of '94, Jordan broke into the Scorpions with a .252 average and six stolen bases. All this after hitting .202 at Birmingham in what was supposed to be preparation for one of the biggest jumps of Jordan's career: the catapult to Triple-A ball that could have come in 1995.

It didn't. Baseball's labor dispute, already having forced the cancellation of the 1994 World Series, finally wore down the greatest basketball player of our time. That, and perhaps the slightest inkling to return to the hardcourt, prompted Jordan's exit from the sport he so briefly graced with his presence. A year later, he was back with the Bulls, making another run to yet another NBA title.

But Jordan's visit to baseball was not soon forgotten. MJ attracted a whole new audience to minor league stadiums. Sure, you can see celebrities at sporting events on a regular basis.

BY AARON DERR

BASEBALL YEARS 1994-1995

74 EVERYTHING YOU NEED TO KNOW ABOUT

1994-1995 BASEBALL YEARS

Heavyweight championship bouts, Grand Slam tennis events or just about any NBA game feature their share of famous fans, but only when Michael played baseball did the stars come out to see minor league games.

During the Barons' first two home games with Jordan on the roster, TV host Kathie Lee Gifford and singer/actor Kenny Rogers visited the ballpark. All in all, more than 200,000 fans poured in to watch Michael take his hacks at that ever-elusive hardball.

And when Jordan left the diamond, baseball lost a legend, although in an entirely different way than it will when the inevitable day comes that Cal Ripken Jr. walks away. Pretty much all that's left of Michael's baseball-playing days is a short checklist of cards. Among others, Upper Deck features him in its Organization Profiles, and Action Packed offered the Michael Jordan Scouting Report.

It's probably a safe bet that 10 years ago, few collectors could ever have imagined a Michael Jordan basketball card valued at $2,500 (such as the 1997-98 Upper Deck UD3 Season Ticket Autograph #MJ). Even more far-fetched: the thought of forking up $5,000 for a 1995 SP Minors Autograph Michael Jordan baseball card.

1994-1995 BASEBALL YEARS

After 13 months of promising progress, the world's most recognizable minor leaguer walked away from the uncertainties of baseball

See Ya, Mike

Just like that, it was over.

In the beginning, there were secret hitting lessons underneath Comiskey Park, and afternoons spent fielding groundballs on a gymnasium floor.

In the end, there was a man flying in his private jet over Ed Smith Stadium bidding farewell to baseball in plane language.

For 13 months, Michael Jordan captivated a nation with his bizarre venture into the land of cleats and chewing tobacco.

He failed more than he succeeded, yet converted a legion of sharp-tongued critics. He had more good times than bad, but walked away because the game wouldn't cooperate.

And now he's gone.

For good.

"It was interesting, wasn't it?" White Sox general manager Ron Schueler said in the spring of 1995.

When Schueler made the announcement on Feb. 7, 1994, that Jordan had been signed to a minor league contract, the sporting world shuddered. And snickered.

Jordan showed up at spring training 1994 with a heavy commitment to a game he hadn't played in 14 years. His famed work ethic, brought over from the NBA, was all he had. With a huge media gathering charting every swing, and record-breaking crowds showing up wherever the Sox played, it took Jordan nearly two weeks to get his first single.

By Dan Bickley

"I just didn't know what to expect," Jordan said of his second career. "I was totally lost. There were a lot of expectations, a lot of focus placed on me. But the first day of camp, I'm facing [pitcher] Jose DeLeon, and he's throwing me a knuckle-curve. Like I even knew what one was."

After hitting .150 in 13 spring training games, Jordan was assigned to Double-A Birmingham in the Southern League. He bought a $250,000 bus — the Jordan Cruiser — to serve him and his new teammates. And the day before he left spring training for the first time, he leaned back in his chair in the Sox's clubhouse, smoking a cigar.

"This is going to be the best summer of my life."

BASEBALL YEARS 1994-1995

Before heading to Birmingham, Jordan was named MVP of the Windy City Classic at Wrigley Field, going 2-for-5 with two RBI against the Cubs. And in his first month as a minor leaguer, Jordan's average climbed to .333, and he ranked seventh in Southern League hitting.

But he knew it couldn't last. "I was not a .300 hitter," Jordan said.

Reality began to sink in and, inevitably, the game and Jordan's lack of experience caught up with him, as his batting average plummeted to .178.

But in the stretch run of his rookie season, Jordan came alive. He hit his first home run on Aug. 1, then pointed to the sky as he touched home plate, a tribute to his slain father. He batted .260 during the final month of the season, hitting two more homers to finish the season with a .202 average.

The Jordan line: He tied for the team lead in games played (127), ranked second in stolen bases (30) and fourth in RBI (51). All in all, not a bad year. Actually, a darn good year for a guy who hadn't played organized ball since high school.

"The average was about what we expected," Schueler said. "But the RBI and stolen bases were amazing. No one expected that."

Buoyed by his late-season surge, Jordan earned assignment in the Arizona Fall League. In 35 games, Jordan hit .252 with four doubles, one triple, eight RBI and six stolen bases. Suddenly, his dream of playing in the major leagues wasn't so farfetched after all.

Jordan returned to spring training in February, convinced he had a shot to make the Sox's Opening Day lineup. And from the start, he impressed everyone in the organization. Jordan's bat speed was improving steadily, and he was driving the ball all over the field. In the Sox's intrasquad game, Jordan singled in his first at-bat of the spring.

Yet Jordan suddenly was drawn into the middle of baseball's labor unrest. The players' union asked him not to play in any exhibition games, and he agreed. But Schueler told him he had to move out of the clubhouse and dress in the minor league locker room with everyone else obeying the union.

Jordan immediately cleaned out his locker, and went and played 18 holes of golf with Lamont. Then he boarded a plane the next morning, circled the Sox's facility, and headed back to Chicago.

No more. Just like that, his baseball career was finished. More than likely, Jordan had decided that he was not going to spend another season in the minor leagues. He was going to make the Sox's Opening Day roster or walk away for good. And the labor strife made it impossible for him to fulfill that plan.

Nevertheless, it was fun. While it lasted.

"It was a memorable experience," Schueler said. "I think Jordan learned a lot, and I think he showed how tough it is to play this game.

"But everyone here learned from his work ethic, and the way he approached every game. We learned from each other and that's good."

Dan Bickley took time out in 1995 from his White Sox beat work for the Chicago Sun Times to write about Jordan for **Beckett Baseball Card**

1994-1995 BASEBALL YEARS

Price Guide

Baseball Cards
1994-95

Values were full retail selling prices at the time of publication.

All cards are valued in Mint condition.

BASEBALL YEARS 1994-1995

1991

Set	No.	Price
Upper Deck	SP1	15.00

1992-97

Set	No.	Price
Sports Illustrated For Kids II	270	10.00

1994

Set	No.	Description	Price
Action Packed	23		5.00
Birmingham Barons Classic	23		15.00
Birmingham Barons Fleer/ProCards	633		10.00
Classic	1		3.00
Collector's Choice	635		2.50
Collector's Choice	661	RC	6.00
Collector's Choice Gold Signature	635	UP	80.00
Collector's Choice Gold Signature	661		160.00
Collector's Choice Silver Signature	635	UP	10.00
Collector's Choice Silver Signature	661	RC	25.00
Fun Pack	170	RC	10.00
SP Previews	CR2		40.00
SP Holoviews	16		40.00
SP Holoviews Die Cuts	16		300.00
Ted Williams Dan Gardiner Collection	DG1		25.00
Upper Deck	19		RC 10.00
Upper Deck Electric Diamond	19 RC		40.00
Upper Deck Diamond Collection	C2		50.00
Upper Deck Next Generation	8		40.00
Upper Deck Next Generation Electric Diamond	8		50.00
Upper Deck The American Epic	BC2 (Direct mail insert)		5.00
Upper Deck Minors	MJ23	Gold	70.00
Upper Deck Minors	MJ23	Silver	20.00

1995

Set	No.	Price
Collector's Choice	500	2.50
Collector's Choice Gold Signature	500	60.00
Collector's Choice Silver Signature	500	10.00
Collector's Choice SE	238	4.00
Collector's Choice SE Gold Signature	238	150.00
Collector's Choice SE Silver Signature	238	16.00
SP Minors Autographs	14	5000.00
SP Minors Michael Jordan Time Capsule	TC1	8.00
SP Minors Michael Jordan Time Capsule	TC2	8.00
SP Minors Michael Jordan Time Capsule	TC3	8.00
SP Minors Michael Jordan Time Capsule	TC4	8.00
Upper Deck	200	3.00
Upper Deck Electric Diamond	200	12.00
Upper Deck Electric Diamond Gold	200	125.00
Upper Deck Steal of a Deal	SD15	30.00
Upper Deck Michael Jordan One On One	1 Throwing	1.00
Upper Deck Michael Jordan One On One	2 Fielding	1.00
Upper Deck Michael Jordan One On One	3 Hitting	1.00

1994-1995 BASEBALL YEARS

Upper Deck Michael Jordan One On One	4 Speed	1.00
Upper Deck Michael Jorda One On One	5 Overall Skills	1.00
Upper Deck Michael Jordan One On One	6 '94 Spring	1.00
Upper Deck Michael Jordan One On One	7 '94 Season	1.00
Upper Deck Michael Jordan One On One	8 First Homer	1.00
Upper Deck Michael Jordan One On One	9 '94 Autumn	1.00
Upper Deck Michael Jordan One On One	10 The Future	1.00
Upper Deck Minors	45	3.00
Upper Deck Minors Future Stock	45	12.00
Upper Deck Minors Michael Jordan's Scrapbook	MJ1 Decisions	18.00
Upper Deck Minors Michael Jordan's Scrapbook	MJ2 Practice	18.00
Upper Deck Minors Michael Jordan's Scrapbook	MJ3 Spring Training and Assignment	18.00
Upper Deck Minors Michael Jordan's Scrapbook	MJ4 Windy City Classic	18.00
Upper Deck Minors Michael Jordan's Scrapbook	MJ5 Firsts	18.00
Upper Deck Minors Michael Jordan's Scrapbook	MJ6 The Hitting Streak	18.00
Upper Deck Minors Michael Jordan's Scrapbook	MJ7 Struggles	18.00
Upper Deck Minors Michael Jordan's Scrapbook	MJ8 Life on the Road	18.00
Upper Deck Minors Michael Jordan's Scrapbook	MJ9 Firs Home Run	18.00
Upper Deck Minors Michael Jordan's Scrapbook	MJ10 Arizona Fall League	18.00
Upper Deck Minors Michael Jordan Season Highlights Jumbos	MJ1 White Sox welcome Jordan to Spring Training	5.00
Upper Deck Minors Michael Jordan Season Highlights Jumbos	MJ2 Jordan supplies offense at Classic	5.00
Upper Deck Minors Michael Jordan Season Highlights Jumbos	MJ3 Jordan extends hitting streak	5.00
Upper Deck Minors Michael Jordan Season Highlights Jumbos	MJ4 Jordan hits first home run	5.00
Upper Deck Minors Michael Jordan Season Highlights Jumbos	MJ5 Extracurricular baseball	5.00
Upper Deck Minors Organizational Profiles	OP6	25.00

HOW TO COLLECT JORDAN AUTOGRAPHS

How to Collect Jordan Autographs

By Steve Wilson

The news in the summer of 1998 reverberated out of Chicago with all the force of a Michael Jordan slam dunk. At the National Sports Collectors Convention, Upper Deck won the auction bidding for a Jordan game-used 1992-93 road Bulls uniform. The price was a whopping $26,000.

Then came the aftershock. Memorabilia collectors nationwide cringed when they heard what the California company planned to do with the prized gamer: Cut it into pieces. The swatches would then be signed by The Man himself and used to decorate a chase set.

It's a good thing Upper Deck employees didn't just unsheathe scissors and start cutting away. That would be too much to handle. Instead, collectors can console themselves with the hope of pulling or purchasing one of the jersey cards.

The dream lives on: to actually own a Jordan game-used jersey. But the reality falls in the happy medium between the ultimate — a gamer — and a cloth-coated insert card. The supplier is Upper Deck Authenticated, the card company's sports memorabilia branch whose contract with the Bulls' megastar allows it to be the biggest outlet of authentic Jordan-signed merchandise.

Yet it seems no outlet is big enough to satisfy the demand for everything Michael. In the winter of 1987, UDA was forced to stop — at least momentarily — taking orders from customers

MICHAEL JORDAN COLLECTIBLES **83**

HOW TO COLLECT JORDAN AUTOGRAPHS

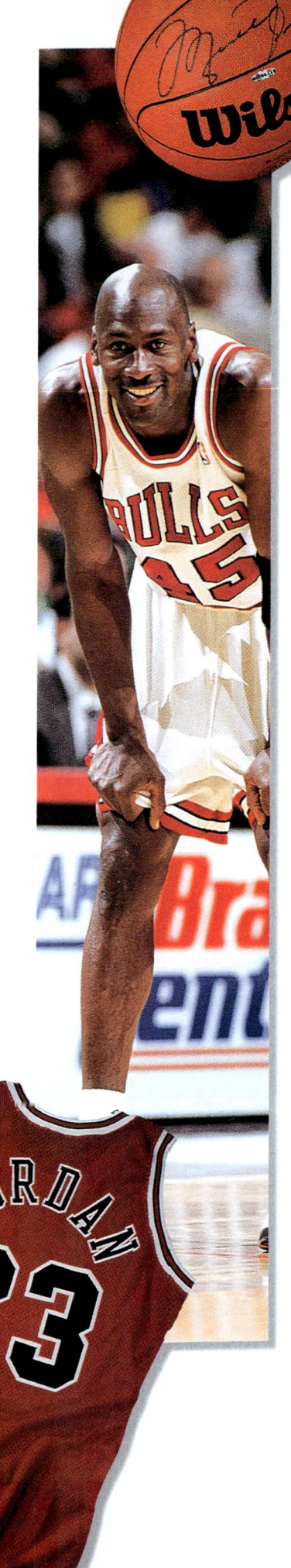

for any more signed Jordan items. Jordan, you see, couldn't sign fast enough to keep up with an overwhelming demand, and UDA's supply had been drained dry.

From the time he arrived, Jordan's been UDA's main man. Officials won't say how much money in sales No. 23 brings in annually, but it's clear that he's the runaway leader in a stable of superstars. His Airness produces three of the five best sellers: No. 1, signed jersey; No. 2, signed basketball; and No. 5, signed 16-by-20 photograph of him in the 1987 Slam Dunk Championship. Autographed jerseys of Griffey and Joe Montana rank third and fourth, respectively.

Other Jordan-signed items run from commemorative baseball jerseys and a Bulls No. 45 jersey (marking his return to the NBA) to Upper Deck's own line of Mr. June products.

Collectors happily pay three and four figures for many of the UDA pieces. Full selling prices for non-UDA signed pieces in Mint condition are $100 for photos, $550 for authentic jerseys, $400 for NBA balls, $275 for indoor/outdoor balls, $325 for replica jerseys, and about $60 for trading cards.

With such high values at stake, there's plenty of incentive to make sure a signed piece is authentic.

"I've seen a bunch of counterfeit items," says no higher authority than Michael himself. "I can look at an item right away and know if it's legit just by the signature.

"I sign a little [apart from UDA], but I always put 'Best Wishes,' which separates that from what I do for Upper Deck."

84 EVERYTHING YOU NEED TO KNOW ABOUT

HOW TO COLLECT JORDON AUTOGRAPHS

PRICE GUIDE

Autographed Memorabilia

Values were full retail selling prices at the time of publication, but it should be
noted that lower prices can be found through extensive shopping.

HOW TO COLLECT JORDAN AUTOGRAPHS

HOW TO COLLECT JORDAN AUTOGRAPHS

UDA SIGNED JERSEYS

1992-93	Bulls Jersey #23 Red Unframed	1800.00
1992-93	Bulls Jersey #23 White Unframed	1800.00
11/1/94	Retired Jersey Unframed/111	4500.00
1994-95	Bulls Jersey #45 Red Unframed	4500.00
1994-95	Bulls Jersey #45 Red Framed	4700.00
1995-96	Bulls Jersey #23 Black Unframed	1300.00
1995-96	Bulls Jersey #23 Red Unframed	1300.00
1995-96	Bulls Jersey #23 White Unframed	1300.00
1996-97	Bulls Jersey #23 Red Unframed	1200.00
1996-97	Bulls Jersey #23 Red Framed	1400.00
1996-97	Bulls Jersey #23 White Unframed	1200.00
1996-97	Bulls Jersey #23 White Framed	1400.00
1996-97	Bulls Jersey #23 Black Unframed	1200.00
1996-97	Bulls Jersey #23 Black Framed	1400.00
Bulls 72-10 Black Jersey Framed/72		5500.00
Mr. June Red Jersey Unframed/423		2100.00
Retro Jersey with 1984-85 Design Framed/50		6250.00
Mr. June White Jersey Framed/423		2800.00
Mr. June Red Jersey Framed/423		2300.00
Birmingham Barons Jersey Framed/250		3000.00
Birmingham Barons Jersey Unframed/250		2800.00
Space Jam Jersey Unframed		4000.00
1997-98	Nike Bulls Jersey #23 Black Unframed	1800.00
1997-98	Nike Bulls Jersey #23 White Unframed	1800.00
1997-98	Nike Bulls Jersey #23 Red Unframed	1800.00

UDA SIGNED PHOTOS

16x20	Crying With Trophy Framed	850.00
16x20	Crying With Trophy Unframed	800.00
16x20	Flying Framed	850.00
16x20	Flying Unframed	800.00
16x20	Slam Dunk Framed/1000	850.00
16x20	Slam Dunk Unframed/1000	800.00
16x20	Lefty Slam Framed/300	1200.00
16x20	The Dish Framed/300	1200.00
16x20	Golf Framed/230	1200.00
16x20	Mid-Air Slam Framed/300	1200.00
16x20	Jumpman Framed/300	1200.00
16x20	UNC 17 Seconds Framed/750	850.00
16x20	UNC 17 Seconds Unframed/750	800.00
16x20	UNC Dunk Framed	850.00
16x20	UNC Dunk Unframed	800.00
16x20	1997 Champs Framed/230	1000.00
8x10	1988 Slam Dunk Contest Framed	550.00
8x10	First Game Back Unframed	400.00
8x10	Baseball Framed	400.00
8x10	Baseball Unframed	400.00
8x10	Mid-Air Slam Unframed/1200	550.00
8x10	1988 Slam Dunk Contest Unframed	500.00
Mr. June Collection w/letter #1/423		1500.00
Mr. June Collection w/letter #2/423		1100.00
1995-96 Championship Season Photo Collection Framed/72		1000.00

OTHER UDA SIGNED ITEMS

Black Baseball Bat/500	1500.00
Chicago Stadium Floor w/8x10 Framed/1000	1300.00
Danny Day Lithograph/197	2000.00
Rare Air Book w/linen sleeve/2500	500.00
Hand-Painted Basketball/200	1600.00
"I'm Back" Basketball (laser engraved/1995)	1300.00
Indoor/Outdoor Basketball	800.00
Leather "Basketball/Baseball"/1000	650.00

HOW TO COLLECT JORDAN AUTOGRAPHS

Mr. June Black Basketball w/logo/423	1500.00
Nike Wings Poster 12x36 Framed/500	800.00
SI Cover "Star is Born" (12/10/84) Framed	425.00
White Sox Cap/250	500.00
Wilson Baseball	400.00
Wilson Jet Basketball	1300.00
1996 SPx Record Breaker Card/250	500.00
72-Win Basketball/72	1000.00
5x7 Photo w/Replica Floor Piece/72	1000.00

OTHER SIGNED ITEMS (NON-UDA)

1984	Nike Air-Jordan Sneakers From Olympics	2800.00
1986-87	Nike Air-Jordan White/Red/Black Sneakers	2500.00
1990	Gatorade Promotional Mini-Ball	250.00
1995-96	Bulls Championship Banner (28" X 45", 15 Signatures)	2100.00
1995-96	Championship Spalding Basketball (13 Signatures)	1400.00
1995-96	Game Worn Red/White Air Jordan Sneakers (Size 13)	1600.00
1995-96	Warm-Up Jacket and Pants	3200.00

HOW TO COLLECT JORDAN AUTOGRAPHS

REAL AIR

Michael Jordan's autograph is the toughest to land and most likely to be forged

By Mike Breeden

Who's the greatest player in NBA history?

Wilt Chamberlain has his supporters. So does Bill Russell, Larry Bird and Michael Jordan. Get a wide enough range of fans to vote, and it's prob-ably too close to call.

But when it comes to basketball autographs, it's no contest.

Jordan is the unchallenged king in the signature market. Even the elusive Russell, who broke his long-time non-signer status to appear at shows where his fees started at $300 per signature, can't dispute Jordan's claim as the hobby's hottest basketball autograph.

Jordan is in the sixth year of his association with Upper Deck Authen-ticated, the company that pays him big bucks for exclusive rights to his autographed material. UDA has offered various signed items since this contractual relationship began, but many collectors feel that the asking prices are way out of line with the market price.

Personally, I think UDA's prices on Jordan material are the market prices. After all, UDA is the only company with quantities of guaranteed authentic Jordan autographed material. Jordan-signed items that don't originate at Upper Deck Authenticated may be less expensive, but there is a trade-off in terms of guaran-teed authenticity. If you're going to buy a non-UDA item, make sure your

HOW TO COLLECT JORDAN AUTOGRAPHS

purchase comes from a reliable dealer who can demonstrate the provenance of the item, and is willing to back it up with a money-back pledge.

When a signature commands as much interest as does Jordan's, the ethically challenged segment of the hobby usually takes notice in a big way. Forgers have been capitalizing on the demand for Michael by flooding the market with fake Jordan autographs for several years now.

Recently, one crook was arrested after an FBI investigation uncovered hundreds of forged autographs. Many of the phony sigs were Jordans, and they were found on a variety of items, including basketballs and jerseys.

In an apparently unrelated incident, stacks of plaques featuring "signed" photos of Jordan wearing uniform No. 45 were being sold on street corners in Chicago shortly after his return from retirement. Believe me, no one obtains a supply like this legitimately. Remember, if a deal seems too good to be true, it probably is.

Jordan himself has made life a little easier for the forgers by changing his signature over the years. When he first entered the league, you could make out almost every letter in his name. These days, an M and a J along with a series of lines comprise most of his signatures. He rarely takes the time to spell out his entire name any more, thereby reducing the efforts that forgers have to put into falsifying his signature.

So, if buying a pre-signed item is fraught with peril, why not just go out and get it yourself? Unfortunately, your chances of getting MJ to personally sign an item are about as good as the chances of you being signed to an NBA contract by Bulls owner Jerry Reinsdorf.

Writing to Jordan in hopes of getting an autograph in the mail has been an exercise in futility for just about as long as he's been in the NBA. He simply gets too much mail to think about opening, let alone answering, it all. That comes with the territory when you're among the world's most recognizable faces.

Your chances of getting Jordan's autograph in person are only slightly better.

Given the constant demand he faces, it's clear why Jordan rarely stops to sign. Even catching him in his Chicago restaurant is unlikely to increase your chances. He has, however, been more receptive to requests from people who wish only to shake his hand or have their picture taken with him.

So it's obvious getting a guaranteed authentic Jordan autograph is going to cost you some money, one way or another. You can either follow him around from city to city and hope to catch him in a rare signing moment, or you can buy one that has the Upper Deck Authenticated name on it.

Sure, you're likely to see Jordan-signed photos around for less than $50. But the chances of something this inexpensive being authentic are about the same as opponents had trying to slow down Chamberlain in his prime — the odds are against you. I suggest playing it safe.

Mike Breeden is publisher of The Autograph Hound newsletter (804-346-8775) based in Glen Allen, Va.

WHEN REQUESTING AUTOGRAPHS OF YOUR FAVORITE ATHLETES THROUGH THE MAIL, ALWAYS INCLUDE A SASE – SELF-ADDRESSED STAMPED ENVELOPE. AND DON'T FORGET THE STAMP!

HOW TO COLLECT JORDAN AUTOGRAPHS

SINCE SIGNING MICHAEL JORDAN TO AN EXCLUSIVE CONTRACT, UPPER DECK AUTHENTICATED HAS BEEN . . .

FLYING HIGH

By Bob Brill

One of the most important decisions made by the Upper Deck Company and Upper Deck Authenticated was to lock Michael Jordan into a reported 10-year, multi-million dollar contract for cards and memorabilia.

The decision was more important financially than even the benchmark of picturing Ken Griffey Jr. on the very first Upper Deck card. While Griffey is arguably the best player in baseball heading into the 21st century, Jordan is arguably the best basketball player of all time.

"I think Michael Jordan clearly has transcended trading cards, memorabilia and basketball itself and he's done a lot of great things for collecting in general," of Howard Farfel at Upper Deck said in 1997. "He's expanded the collector base because people who are big-time sports fans who may not have been collectors, want anything that is Michael Jordan."

Jordan is in the middle of his 10-year relationship with UDA and in these times of surging memorabilia sales and a shrinking card market, Jordan's Upper Deck exclusivity is looming larger than ever.

While hyped rookies come and go, the one constant in basketball remains Michael Jordan. Upper Deck even capitalized in a big way when Air Jordan left the NBA to pursue a career in baseball.

The other companies who wanted to have Jordan in their minor league baseball sets had to bow before Upper Deck to include him. The rules were

92 EVERYTHING YOU NEED TO KNOW ABOUT

HOW TO COLLECT JORDAN AUTOGRAPHS

laid out stringently. If another card company wanted to include Michael Jordan as a minor league baseball player in its set, the company had to treat him as a common. Only Upper Deck could advertise him and only Upper Deck could place him in an insert series.

Jordan's exclusive contract applies to basketball cards, too. If a card company wants to put a player on its packs or on boxes for advertising, it won't be Jordan. Only Upper Deck has that privilege. That is why in most cases and in all cases involving premium or super premium class cards, it is Jordan on the cover. Simply put: Jordan sells.

Farfel says people recognize Jordan on a pack of trading cards at the grocery store and it appeals to them. If they buy the pack of cards, Jordan's likeness on the wrapper may be the reason why.

With Upper Deck's Meet the Stars program, in which one lucky fan will get to spend time with the superstar, the California-based company really has struck gold.

"The ability to use Jordan in Meet the Stars has been huge," Farfel said. "The grand prize winner gets to meet Jordan and there is not a better prize out there. He's paid big dividends."

Bob Brill, who owns a card shop in California, also works as a freelance writer and media relations consultant.

HOW TO COLLECT JORDAN AUTOGRAPHS

The Day Jordan Was Stopped

No, not by anyone in the NBA, silly, but by Upper Deck Authenticated

Can there ever be too much of a good thing when it comes to memorabilia autographed by the world's most famous athlete?

If you're Upper Deck Authenticated, the card company's sports memorabilia branch whose contract with the Bulls' megastar allows it to be the biggest outlet of authentic Jordan signed merchandise in the collectibles industry, the answer is "yes."

No, seriously. The answer's "yes."

It seems Jordan's incredible popularity is such that last winter UDA was forced to stop — at least momentarily — taking orders from customers for any more signed Jordan items. Jordan, you see, couldn't sign fast enough to keep up with an overwhelming demand, and UDA's supply had been drained dry.

By Randy Cummings

HOW TO COLLECT JORDAN AUTOGRAPHS

"I've been here for about three and a half years, and when I first started, Jordan was popular — he was probably in our top three in terms of units sold," UDA's Brenton Demko told *Beckett* in 1998. "Now, we probably have a 10- to 12-month waiting list for Jordan items on back order. We used to have stock on the guy. Now, you have to wait 10 months."

From the time he arrived, Jordan's been UDA's main man. Officials won't say how much money in sales No. 23 brings in annually, but it's clear that he's the runaway leader in a stable of superstars such as Ken Griffey Jr., Troy Aikman and Wayne Gretzky UDA has under contract to sign memorabilia ranging from jerseys, bats and balls to helmets, shoes and exclusive commemorative items.

And so last November, UDA reached the point where it finally had to step back and stop taking orders for Jordan signed items. Michael's contract spells out a specific number (UDA won't say how many) of autographs he's required to provide and when the back log of orders got out of hand, the company had to, in effect, start turning away business.

"We're currently not accepting orders for Jordan items," Demko said at the time. "We curtailed orders so Jordan could catch up."

(Note to readers: The preceding paragraph is probably worth another read.)

Not that UDA is whining about the situation. Company officials know what they've got in Jordan, and they're proud that most hobbyists

HOW TO COLLECT JORDAN AUTOGRAPHS

HOW TO COLLECT JORDAN AUTOGRAPHS

realize that to obtain an authenticated autograph of Jordan, they're probably going to have to go through UDA to get it.

"He's definitely our No. 1 athlete," Upper Deck's Mark Christenson said in Spring 1998. "His popularity and celebrity have been instrumental in building our company.

"We signed him in 1994, and he immediately went to the forefront of our sales," he added. "Of course, everybody who has associated with him has experienced increases in their sales."

Jordan's signature on Bulls jerseys and NBA basketballs (see related box) remain the company's top-selling items. But he's also featured on photos, magazine covers and any number of various items that include commemorative baseball jerseys from his attempts to play in the bigs and a Bulls No. 45 jersey marking his return to the NBA, to Upper Deck's own line of Mr. June products.

"There are a lot of specialty pieces we do for him," Christenson said.

Jordan's popularity — who doesn't want an MJ autograph? — extends beyond his adoring public. Even some of UDA's other superstar clients have asked for signed Jordan memorabilia through the company's access to His Airness. When Aikman signed on with the company, for example, he quickly sought a Jordan autograph. Gretzky and Dan Marino are others who used their ties with UDA to get items signed by Jordan.

"I got some Michael stuff," said Marino, the Miami Dolphins QB. "You know what it is, we just kind of trade off everything — [Jordan] and everybody. They give me all those things, and I put 'em away for the kids."

Added Christenson: "We'll do that from time to time. Some of the guys will want something or maybe they have a child who wants something."

As Demko will tell you, these days just about everybody wants something with Jordan's autograph on it.

Hey, he's got the back log of orders to prove it.

Randy Cummings is a former editor of **Becket Basketball Card Monthly.**

MISCELLANEOUS

Who wouldn't want Michael Jordan in their starting lineup?

Kenner certainly did when it tipped off its NBA Starting Lineups series of figures featuring Jordan in 1988. And although the run came to an end after 1993 due to licensing complications, the Kenner SLUs have since become quite the collectible.

Warner Brothers certainly wanted MJ in its lineup, and although few will mistake him for Denzel Washington, when the world's most recognizable athlete hit the big screen it was hard not to stand up and take notice. Jordan's entertaining turn alongside Bugs Bunny and other Looney Tunes in the 1996 major motion picture "Space Jam" spawned a whole new genre of collectibles, from an Asteroid Crater Golf Set valued at $18 to Michael Jordan Cologne worth about $75.

Big-time corporations such as Nike and Gatorade love having Michael in their lineup of spokesmen. Now promotional items featuring Jordan's likeness are finding homes in collections everywhere. An original Gatorade "Life is a Sport" poster will run collectors around $15, and an original Nike Advertising vinyl banner is worth $25.

Basically, if it has anything to do with Michael Jordan, somebody, somewhere out there, wants it. And you'd be hard-pressed to find anything with more overall appeal than the Starting Lineups.

Kenner introduced Jordan in its inaugural SLU basketball set in 1988 as part of a three-piece Chicago Bulls team set that also featured John Paxson and Scottie Pippen. All three were clad in their white Bulls uniforms with red trim, and that first Jordan figure will go for $110 these days. The Jordan collector card and the figure both featured Michael with hair, something many younger collectors might not remember. The Bulls' team cases contained 12 figures, most of which were Jordan issues, and were distributed on a nationwide basis.

In addition, Jordan appeared in the 1988 SLU NBA Slam Dunk red-and-white boxed set along with such notables as Magic Johnson, Larry Bird, Charles Barkley, Patrick Ewing, Isiah Thomas and Dominque Wilkins. Because of the apparent surplus of

MISCELLANEOUS

MISCELLANEOUS

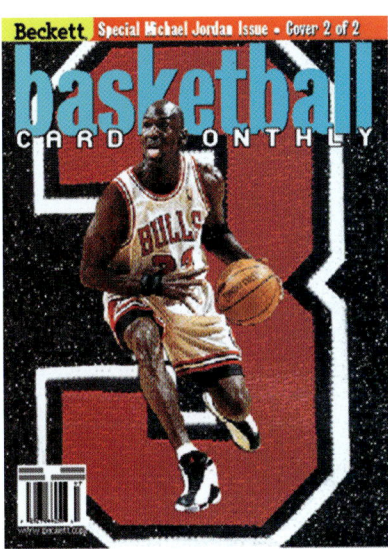

Nobody graces a magazine front like Michael. The most popular athlete on the planet has been a favorite coverboy of *Beckett Basketball Card Monthly* for years. With his credentials, can you blame us?

MISCELLANEOUS

Jordan SLU figures in 1988, many collectors left Michael behind on store shelves while pursuing more difficult regional issues in hopes of completing the 85-piece set.

Kenner abandoned its plans for a 106-piece 1989 Basketball issue after releasing just three Charlotte Hornets and two Cleveland Cavaliers. Five Bulls, including Jordan, were included in that pre-release list. Jordan did appear, however, in Kenner's 1989 One on One series, which featured two players on one base posed in the heat of the hardcourt battle. Jordan is matched against Isiah Thomas in a driving layup pose.

Another Jordan SLU appearance came in 1990 as part of a 17-player release. Two collector cards accommodated the Jordan figure, which is clad in the Bulls' red uniform. The regular issue card depicts Michael in one of his patented slam dunk positions, while the "rookie year" card has a short biographical sketch on the reverse. Like the 1988 rookie issue, Jordan once again has a full head of hair.

Two Jordan SLU issues appeared on retail store shelves in 1991. Both were issued as part of the 16-player release. Both feature Jordan in his white Bulls uniform and, for the first time, without hair. Each figure has its own unique collector card but both share the same collector coin with identical biographical sketches on one side and Jordan's likeness on the other.

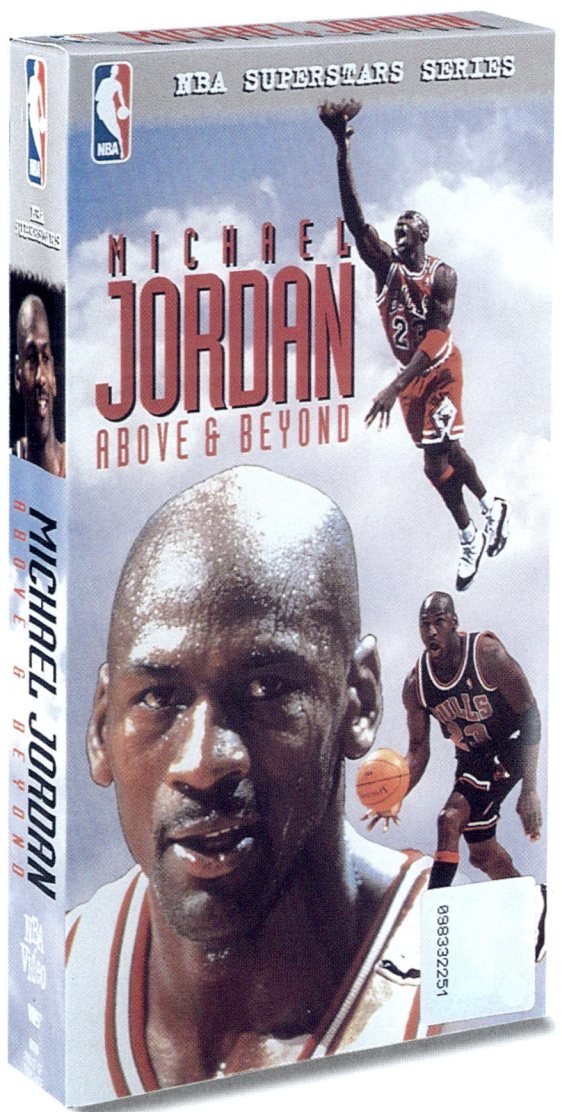

Michael Jordan's final appearance in the Starting Lineup line came in 1993 as a part of the 29-piece set. The "retirement" Jordan, as it often is referred to, became the final Jordan piece produced by Kenner and is also the most valuable, booking at $200. The 1993 Jordan edition came with a regular issue Topps card and a Topps Stadium Club card, both of which feature the Starting Lineup trademark logo. The figure reveals Jordan in his reverse slam dunk pose reminiscent of his "rookie" release of 1988.

MICHAEL JORDAN COLLECTIBLES

MISCELLANEOUS

PRICE GUIDE

Miscellaneous

Values were full retail selling prices at the time of publication, but it should be noted that lower prices can be found through extensive shopping.

MISCELLANEOUS

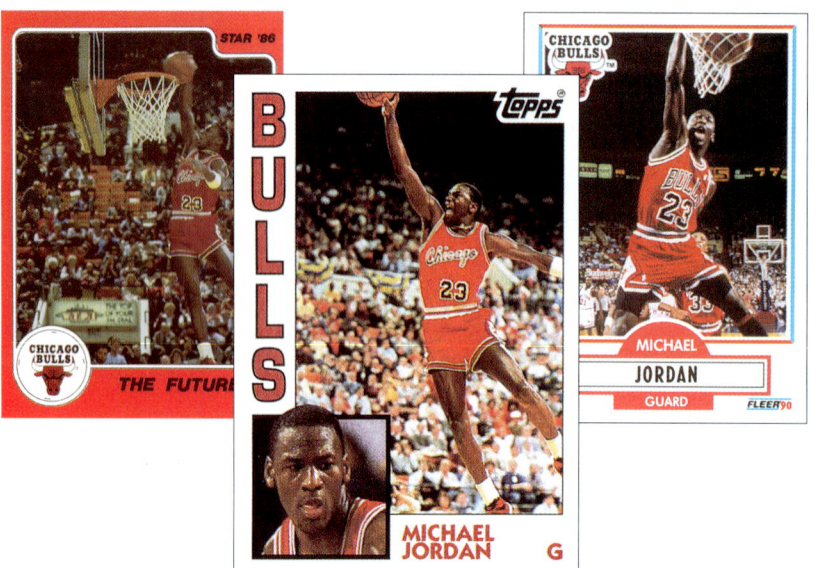

ADVERTISING

Year	Item	Price
1985	Guy Laroche Wristwatch Cardboard Sign (9 x 12)	150.00
1985	World Book Poster	35.00
1988	Wilson Window Poster	30.00
1993	Chicago Sun Times Team Poster	25.00
1993	Chicago Tribune Blow-up "Threepeat"	12.00
1993	Gatorade 3-D Standee Sign	75.00
1993	Gatorade Promotional Poster	20.00
1993	Nike MJ/Spike Lee Mars Blackman Poster	20.00
1994	Hanes Promotional Poster	20.00
1995	Gatorade "Life is a Sport" Poster	15.00
1995	Nike Advertising Vinyl Banner	55.00
1996	Chevy/Geo Poster	25.00
1997	Space Jam Video Cardboard Display	25.00

BULLS TEAM-PRODUCED

Year	Item	Price
1984-85	Media Guide	60.00
1984-85	Pocket Schedule	40.00
1984-85	Season Ticket Pamphlet	80.00
1984-85	Yearbook*	90.00
1985-86	Media Guide	40.00
1985-86	Season Ticket Brochure	40.00
1986-87	Media Guide	35.00
1986-87	Pocket Schedule	18.00
1986-87	Season Ticket Pamphlet	100.00
1986-87	Team Calendar	35.00
1987-88	Media Guide*	5.00
1987-88	Yearbook	75.00
1987-88	Pocket Schedule	15.00
1987-88	Team Calendar	20.00
1988-89	Media Guide*	40.00
1988-89	Yearbook*	50.00
1989-90	Pocket Schedule	10.00
1989-90	Yearbook	35.00
1990-91	Media Guide*	25.00

MISCELLANEOUS

1990-91	Yearbook*	30.00
1990-91	25th Ann. Team Calendar	25.00
1990-91	Pocket Schedule	6.00
1990-91	Team Photo (8 x 10)	15.00
1991-92	Team Photo	15.00
1991-92	Yearbook*	30.00
1992-93	Media Guide*	20.00
1992-93	Pocket Schedule	12.00
1992-93	Team Photo	15.00
1993-94	Yearbook*	25.00
1995-96	Pocket Schedule	5.00
1995-96	Team Photo	15.00
1995-96	Yearbook*	20.00
1996-97	Media Guide*	15.00
1996-97	"Ring Award" Photo	15.00
1996-97	Team Calendar	15.00
1996-97	Yearbook*	20.00
1997-98	Team Photo	15.00

EPHEMERA

1982	NCAA Final Four UNC Pennant	45.00
1984	Complete Ticket From Jordan's First Game (10/19)	800.00
1985	Guy Larouch Wristwatch	150.00
1986	Bill Clark Lithograph (16 x 20)	95.00
1987	Coca Cola Vending Machine Decal	20.00
1989	NBA All-Star Game Caricature	15.00
1990-91	"World Champions" Team Photo Button (3-1/2 inch)	12.00
1991	Cleo Valentines in the Box (11)	10.00
1992	Cleo Valentines Greeting Card Puzzle	9.00
1992	Complete Game Ticket (12/4)	30.00
1992	Dream Team Calendar	20.00
1992	RMCC Celebrity Golf Classic Caddy Jacket	100.00
1992	Summer Olympics Caricature Pin	25.00
1994	Ohio Art Farewell Game Tray (11/1)	20.00
1994	Retirement-Day Bag	75.00
1995	Birmingham Barons Pocket Schedule (Chevron)	10.00

MISCELLANEOUS

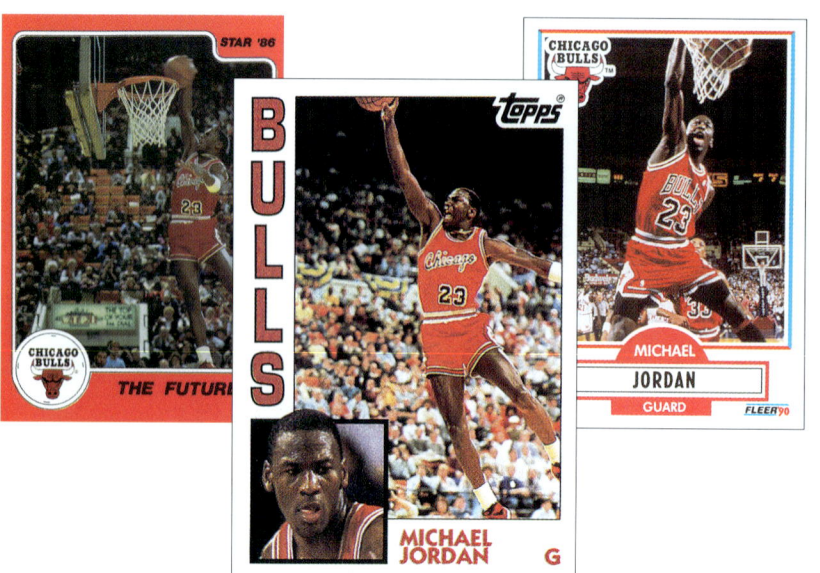

Year	Item	Price
1995-96	Jostens Championship Gold Ring (Sample)	7500.00
1995	RAYOVAC Promotional Brochure	3.00
1996	1996 NBA Playoffs Media Passes (3)	45.00
1996	Applause Inc. Ceramic Mug (Bust)	15.00
1996	Avon Wristwatch in the Box	50.00
1996	Hanes Phone Card Order Form	2.00
1996	NBA Eastern Conference Finals Media Pass	50.00
1996	NBA Playoff Program	20.00
1997	Chicago Sun Times Newspaper "Party On"	10.00
1997	Chicago Tribune Newspaper "Enough Said"	10.00
1997	Michael Jordan Cologne Sticker	3.00
1997	NBA Playoffs Media Pass-Michael Jordan Photo	40.00
1997	NBA Playoffs Media Passes (3)	75.00
1998	Restaurant Gift Bag	2.00
1998	Restaurant Gift Catalog	2.00
1998	Restaurant Gift Embroidered Patch	3.00
1998	Restaurant Gift Matchbook	2.00
1980s	Personal Invitation to Opening Night at MJ's Restaurant	50.00
1990s	Organ Donor Booklet	2.00
1990s	Uncut Sheet of UDA St. Vincent Stamps	40.00

FIGURES/GAMES

Kenner Starting Lineup figures from 1988 to 1990 are valued at NrMt condition. MrMt means a piece has minor flaws, such as slight scratches, a small curl in the package or corners with slight touches of wear. SLUs from 1991 are vauled at Mint, making Mint figures from 1988 to 1990 from 125 to 200 percent above listed value.

Year	Item	Price
1988	Kenner Starting Lineup	110.00
1988-89	SLU Slam Dunk Red/White Box	250.00 / 125.00
1990	Kenner Starting Lineup	120.00
1990	Ohio Art Wall Ball in the Box	75.00
1991	Kenner Starting Lineup Jumping	110.00
1991	Kenner Starting Lineup Dunking	110.00
1992	Dream Team 300 Piece Jig-Saw Puzzle	35.00
1992	Kenner Starting Lineup Regular	125.00
1992	Kenner Starting Lineup Warm-ups	125.00
1992	Kenner Starting Lineup Headline Collection	130.00
1993	Kenner Starting Lineup	200.00
1996	Play By Play Space Jam Doll in the Box	25.00
1996	Play By Play Space Jam Talking Doll in the Box	35.00

MISCELLANEOUS

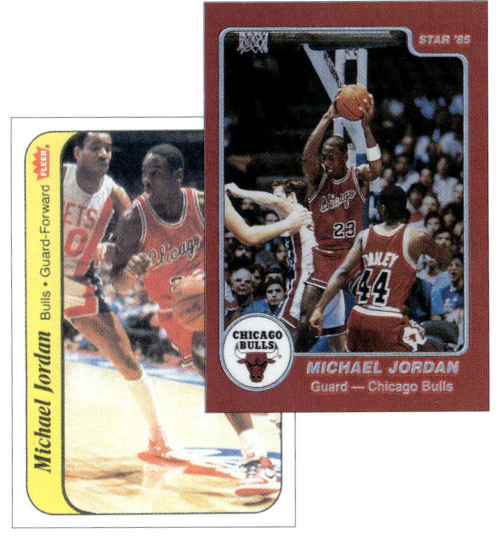

Year	Item	Price
1996	Playmates "Triple Play" Figure Set (3)	40.00
1980s	Ohio Art "Lil Sports" Hoops Set (Miniature)	25.00
1990s	Salvino Figurine (White Jersey)	150.00
1990s	SAM Bobbing Head Figurine	125.00

MCDONALD'S

Year	Item	Price
1986	2-Pocket Homework Folder	15.00
1990	Sports Tips Sheet (8)	15.00
1991	Happy Meal "Fitness Fun" Booklet	10.00
1991	Happy Meal Baseball	15.00
1991	Happy Meal Football	15.00
1991	Happy Meal Frisbee	10.00
1991	Happy Meal Jump-Rope	15.00
1991	Happy Meal Paper Bag	2.00
1991	Happy Meal Stopwatch	10.00
1991	Window Decal	35.00
1993	"Sweet to Repeat" Button (3-inch)	7.00
1997	Tray Liner (Space Jam, French Version)	10.00
1995-96	All-Star Fries Package w/Barkley	10.00
1995-96	French Fry Package w/Bugs Bunny	10.00

PUBLICATIONS
SPORTS ILLUSTRATED

The values are for magazines in ExMt condition. ExMt magazines may have mailing labels or inkjetted addresses if they are otherwise flawless. Magazines without labels or addresses can still be considered ExMt if they have minor flaws, such as dinged/frayed corners, light creases, fingerprints, scratches or scuffing. Both labels or addresses and minor flaws downgrade the condition and value up to 75 percent of listed prices. Flawless issues without labels or addresses are valued at 150 percent of the below prices. * denotes multiplayer front cover.

Date	Cover	Price
11/28/83	M. Jordan/S. Perkins	250.00
7/23/84	Michael Jordan USA	75.00
12/10/84	M.Jordan (1st Bulls cover)	125.00
11/17/86	Michael Jordan	50.00
12/28/87	Year in Pictures	25.00
5/16/88	Michael Jordan	40.00
3/13/89	Michael Jordan	25.00
5/15/89	Michael Jordan	35.00
8/14/89	Michael Jordan golf	25.00
11/6/89	J.Dumars/M.Jordan	35.00

MISCELLANEOUS

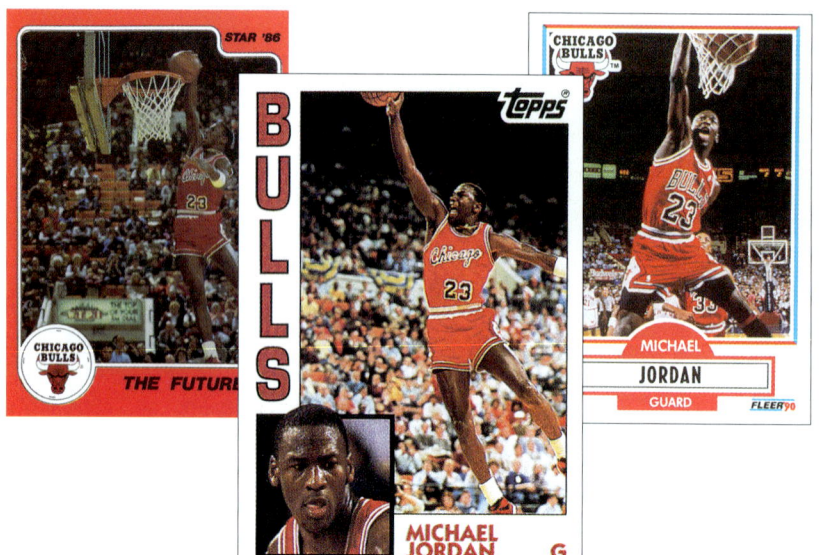

Date	Description	Price
5/21/90	Michael Jordan	35.00
12/17/90	M. Jordan/K. Duckworth	30.00
2/18/91	Dream Team: Jordan, etc.	40.00
6/3/91	Michael Jordan	30.00
6/10/91	M.Johnson/M.Jordan	25.00
6/17/91	Michael Jordan	30.00
8/5/91	Black athlete: Jordan/Joyner	30.00
11/11/91	NBA PV:Jordan/Pippen/Jackson	35.00
12/23/91	Jordan SOY Hologram	40.00
5/11/92	M.Jordan/C.Drexler (FC)	30.00
5/25/92	M. Jordan/P. Ewing	35.00
6/15/92	Michael Jordan	30.00
6/22/92	Michael Jordan	30.00
6/7/93	Michael Jordan	30.00
6/21/93	M.Jordan/C.Barkley	35.00
6/28/93	M.Jordan/S.Pippen	30.00
10/18/93	Michael Jordan "Why?"	30.00
3/14/94	M. Jordan (White Sox)	30.00
3/20/95	Michael Jordan art	25.00
3/27/95	M.Jordan "I'm Back"	25.00
5/22/95	M.Jordan/S.O'Neal	20.00
10/23/95	NBA PV: Rodman/Jordan	20.00
12/31/95	Year in Pictures	20.00
5/27/96	P.Jackson/M.Jordan	15.00
6/3/96	Michael Jordan	15.00
6/17/96	Michael Jordan	15.00
3/10/97	Bulls Cartoon	10.00
6/9/97	Jordan/Rodman	10.00
6/23/97	Michael Jordan	10.00

OTHER PUBLICATIONS

Year	Description	Price
1981	The Sporting News NBA Register	20.00
1983	Basketball Weekly Newspaper (3/24)	65.00
1983	TSN College & Pro Yearbook Magazine*	40.00
1984	Basketball Weekly Newspaper (3/12)	50.00
1984	Basketball Weekly Newspaper (3/19)	50.00
1985	Basketball Digest (June)	40.00
1985	Inside Sport Magazine (Nov.)	20.00
1985	TSN College & Pro Yearbook Magazine	35.00
1985	The Sporting News NBA Guide	30.00
1986	Inside Sport Magazine (Nov.)*	20.00

MISCELLANEOUS

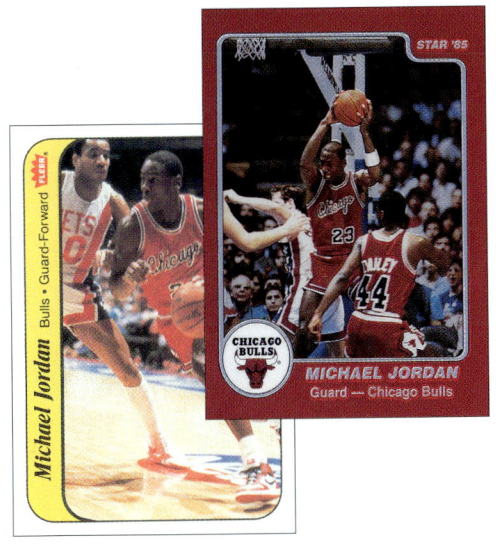

Year	Item	Price
1986	Newsweek "Special Kids" Issue	20.00
1986	Street & Smith's Basketball Yearbook	40.00
1987	Basketball Digest (Jan.)	25.00
1987	Inside Sport Magazine (Dec.)*	30.00
1987	Inside Sport Magazine (June)	40.00
1987	Petersens Pro Basketball Magazine	30.00
1987	TSN College & Pro Yearbook Magazine	30.00
1987	The Sporting News NBA Register	35.00
1988	Basketball Digest (Apr.)	20.00
1988	Basketball Weekly Newspaper (2/15)	30.00
1988	Basketball Weekly Newspaper (2/8)	30.00
1988	Basketball Weekly Newspaper (5/16)	30.00
1988	Inside Sport Magazine (May)*	25.00
1988	Inside Sport Magazine (Nov.)*	25.00
1988	Petersens Pro Basketball Magazine	25.00
1988	Street & Smith's Basketball Yearbook*	25.00
1988	The Sporting News NBA Register	25.00
1989	Basketball Digest (June)	20.00
1989	Basketball Weekly Newspaper (1/16)	30.00
1989	Marketcom Photo Album	25.00
1989	Petersens Pro Basketball Magazine	25.00
1989	Street & Smith's Basketball Yearbook	25.00
1989	TSN College & Pro Yearbook Magazine	20.00
1990	Basketball Digest (Jan.)*	20.00
1990	Basketball Digest (May)	20.00
1990	Basketball Weekly Newspaper (11/13)	20.00
1990	Chicago Sports Profiles Magazine (Nov-Dec.)	7.00
1990	Inside Sport Magazine (Dec.)*	20.00
1990	Inside Sport Magazine (June)	20.00
1990	Inside Sport Magazine (Oct.)	20.00
1990	Petersens Pro Basketball Magazine	20.00
1990	Street & Smith's Basketball Yearbook	20.00
1990	TSN College & Pro Yearbook Magazine	20.00
1991	Atlanta-Press Poster Book	75.00
1991	Basketball Weekly Newspaper (2/25)	20.00
1991	Basketball Weekly Newspaper (5/13)	20.00
1991	Chicago Golfer Magazine	20.00
1991	Chicagoland Cable Guide (May)	15.00
1991	Game Plan Pro Basketball Magazine	20.00
1991	Inside Sport Magazine (May)	20.00
1991	Jet Magazine (7/1)	20.00

MISCELLANEOUS

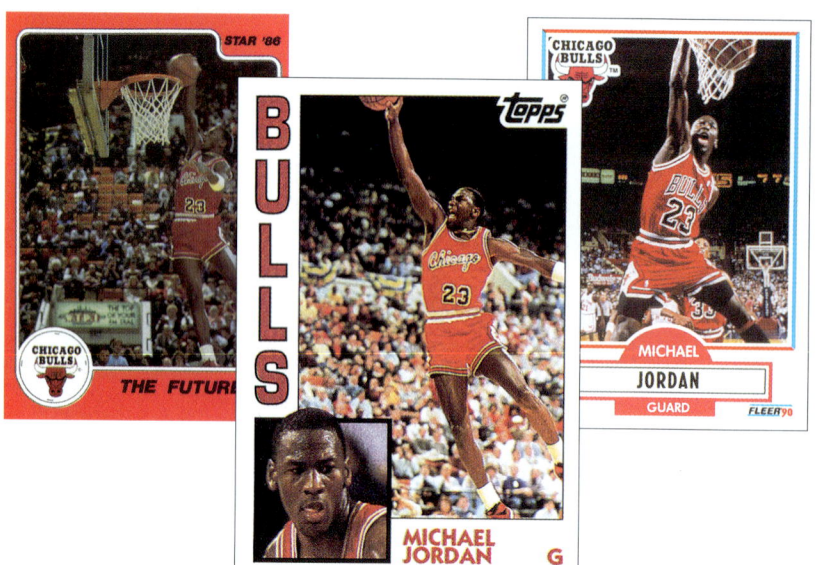

Year	Item	Price
1991	Michael Jordan, MVP And NBA Champ Magazine	10.00
1991	Personality Comic Book "Michael Jordan #6"	5.00
1991	Petersens Pro Basketball Magazine	15.00
1991	Sports Shots Collectors Mini-Book #2	5.00
1991	Street & Smith's Basketball Yearbook	15.00
1992	America's Dynasty "Team USA" Poster Book	20.00
1992	Basketball Weekly Newspaper (5/12)	15.00
1992	Chicago Sports Profiles Magazine (Apr.)	8.00
1992	Inside Sport Magazine (Dec.)*	15.00
1992	Inside Sport Magazine (June)*	15.00
1992	Inside Sport Magazine (Oct.)*	15.00
1992	Jet Magazine (7/6)	20.00
1992	Jet Magazine (8/10)*	15.00
1992	Olympic Men Team Media Guide	50.00
1992	Personality Comic Book "Slam Dunk Kings #1"	5.00
1992	Street & Smith's Basketball Yearbook	15.00
1993	Ebony Magazine (Dec.)	8.00
1993	Jet Magazine (7/12)	15.00
1993	Street & Smith's Basketball Yearbook	15.00
1994	Retirement-Day Program	25.00
1995	NBA Playoff Program*	15.00
1995	Sports & Soaps Magazine (Apr-May)*	12.00
1996	Boom Magazine (Japan)	50.00
1996	Chicago Sports Profiles Magazine (Feb.)	8.00
1996	Marshall Field's Today Magazine	15.00
1996	Walton's Pro Basketball Preview Magazine*	10.00
1997	Basketball Digest (Summer)	5.00
1997	Celebrity Golfer Magazine*	15.00
1997	HBO & Cinemax Magazine (Sept.)	.00
1997	Lazerdisc Magazine (Feb.)	5.00
1983-84	All-Star Sports College Basketball Handbook*	100.00
1985-86	Pro Basketball Illustrated Magazine*	30.00
1985-86	The Sporting News NBA Guide*	30.00
1987-88	Complete Sports Basketball Annual*	20.00
1987-88	Pro Basketball Illustrated Magazine	25.00
1989-90	Panini Sticker Album*	5.00
1989-90	Pro Basketball Illustrated Magazine	20.00
1990-91	NBA Basketball Preview Magazine	25.00

MISCELLANEOUS

1990-91	Rick Barry's Pro Basketball Magazine	20.00
1990-91	Street & Smith's Guide To Pro Basketball	25.00
1991-92	The Sporting News NBA Guide	20.00
1992-93	Complete Sports Basketball Annual*	15.00
1992-93	Panini Sticker Album*	5.00
1995-96	Playoffs Program (Edition #1)*	25.00
1995-96	Street & Smith's Guide To Pro Basketball	15.00
1996-97	NBA Playoff Program	12.00
1996-97	Ultimate Sports Basketball Magazine	10.00

SPACE JAM

Asteroid Crater Golf Set	18.00
Popcorn	10.00
JC Penney Michael Jordan Figurine	150.00
Comforter	45.00
Michael Jordan and Bugs Bunny Figurine	48.00
Hot Hoops Electronic Basketball	35.00
Zero G Basketball	18.00
Snowglobe	22.00
Book Ends	50.00
Talking Michael Jordan	25.00
Gumball Machine	34.00
Ceramic Lamp	45.00
Ceramic Cookie Jar	40.00
Mini mushroom Juvenile Three-Piece Sofa	155.00
Space Jam Hat (Bugs Bunny, Taz, Daffy Duck)	15.00
Michael Jordan and Bugs Bunny Hat	14.00
Space Jam Hat	7.00
Michael Jordan and Elmer Fudd	7.00
Larry Johnson and Barnyard Dog Bupkus	7.00
Michael Jordan and Marvin the Martian	7.00
Michael Jordan and Bugs Bunny	7.00
Charles Barkley and Wile E. Coyote	7.00
Marvin the Martian vs. Nawt	7.00
Yosemite Sam vs. Bupkus	7.00
Taz vs. Blanko	7.00
Michael Jordan and Sylvester	7.00
Daffy Duck vs. Pound	7.00
Michael Jordan Small Figurine	15.00
Michael Jordan Tall Figurine	25.00

MISCELLANEOUS

Michael Jordan Triple Play	20.00
Flag Banner	1.00
Michael Jordan Golf	10.00
Michael Jordan Basketball	10.00
Michael Jordan Baseball	10.00
Monstars: Bang (Green)	7.00
Monstars: Nawt (Pink)	7.00
Monstars: Pound (Orange)	7.00
Monstars: Bupkus (Purple)	7.00
Monstars: Blanko (Blue)	7.00
McDonald's (Lola Bunny, Daffy Duck, Taz, Bugs Bunny, Bupkus, Pound, Blanko)	2.00
Bupkus Small Figurine	2.00
Pound Small Figurine	2.00
Blanko Small Figurine	2.00
Swackhammer and Tweety	7.00
Lola Bunny and Bang	7.00
Michael Jordan and Bugs Bunny Picture	14.00
Tune Squad Picture	14.00
Tune Squad With Michael Picture	14.00
Taz Picture1	4.00
Bugs Bunny Picture	14.00
Daffy Duck Picture	14.00
Michael Jordan (Golf, Basketball, Baseball)	14.00
Space Jam Rug	16.00
Michael Jordan Best of the Best Picture	14.00
Tune Squad and Monstars Picture	14.00
Michael Jordan Pillow	5.00
Michael Jordan Towel Set	20.00
Michael Jordan Sleeping Bag	20.00
Michael Jordan White Coat	86.00
Michael Jordan Shirt	12.00
Michael Jordan Travel Bag	40.00
Michael Jordan Four-Layer Afghan	30.00
Michael Jordan Backpack	13.00
Michael Jordan Winter Pants	12.00
Michael Jordan Pajamas	19.00
Space Jam Underwear	10.00
Space Jam Black Shirt	15.00
Space Jam T-Shirt	15.00
Space Jam Navy-Michael Jordan and Bugs Bunny	44.00

MISCELLANEOUS

Michael Jordan Drape 30.00	Space Jam Electronic Game 30.00
Twin Sheets 20.00	Keywound Alarm 10.00
Michael Jordan Cup 45.00	Koosh: Tweety Bird, Bugs Bunny, Lola Bunny, Taz 10.00
Space Jam Wrapping Paper 3.00	Stars of Space Jam Pictures
Space Jam Poster 6.00	(Daffy Duck, Taz, Sylvester, and Tweety) 15.00
Space Jam Clock 20.00	Swackhammer Jawbreaker 2.00
Michael Jordan Kite 3.00	Lola Bunny, Bugs Bunny Love Dust Candy 2.00
Walkie Talkies 20.00	Paper Plates 3.00
Michael Jordan Tape Cassette 10.00	Paper Cups 2.00
Michael Jordan Upper Deck (18 pack) with MJ figurine 15.00	Stickers 2.00
Space Jam Gold, Silver, and Bronze Coins 110.00	Napkins 2.00
Space Jam Door Hoops 5.00	Slippery Socks 4.00
Space Jam Sipper Straws 3.00	Bandaids 3.00
Three-Piece MJ (Bowl, Cup, and Plate) 11.00	Michael Jordan Gum 1.00
Pocket Basketball Game 15.00	Flashlight 10.00
Lola Bunny Hair Tie 2.00	Bugs Bunny Pen 13.00
Boys Briefs 5.00	Ball Cup Catcher 20.00
Stratos-Slammer Hoop Set 8.00	Space Jam Jello 3.00

MISCELLANEOUS

Macaroni and Cheese	5.00
Over 100 Stickers and Sticker Book	11.00
CD-ROM	35.00
Boxed Set	10.00
Hanes Underwear	5.00
Space Jam Watch	30.00
Candle	3.00
Warner Bros. Gallery Plate	35.00
Shootout Tune Squad Travel Game	15.00
Space Jam Valentine Cards	2.00
Space Jam Picture	25.00
Calendar	12.00
Blanket	6.00
Tape-Soundtrack to Space Jam	12.00
Cards	1.00
Water Bottle	12.00
Muck-Glow in the Dark	6.00
MJ Basketball Press BBall	16.00
Book	5.00
Sports Illustrated for Kids	3.00
Small Space Jam Paperback	3.00
Look to Find Space Jam	5.00
Pull-Out Poster Book	15.00
Coloring Book	5.00
Big Coloring Book	3.00
Bugs	2.00
Invitations	3.00
Banner Party	2.00
Blowouts	3.00
Tattoos	4.00
Wheaties Personalized Jersey Offer	4.00
Reese's Peanut Butter Puffs-Space Jam Boxer	4.00
Boxer Shorts	8.00
Golden Grahams-Free Space Jam Hoop with Ball	4.00
Space Jam Lola Bunny	5.00
Michael Jordan Space Jam Lunch Box	15.00

MISCELLANEOUS

McDonalds Cups (4)	2.00
Outdoor Rubber Ball	5.00
Movie Poster	15.00
Bubble Bath (Bugs Bunny and Daffy Duck)	9.00
Space Jam Bow Biters	5.00
Spalding Lola Bunny Basketball	10.00
Michael Jordan Keychain	5.00
Space Jam Silk Tie	19.00
3-on-3 Basketball Figurine Set	20.00
Michael Jordan Secret Stuff Spring Water	2.00
Space Jam Party Hats	3.00
Frosty Mug	11.00
Michael Jordan Secret Stuff Candy Powder	3.00
Space Jam Shoes	17.00
MJ and Porky Pig Film Card	45.00
MJ and Bugs Gold Film Card (Signed)	45.00
Space Jam Pin (4)	10.00
MJ, Bugs and Marvin the Martian Picture	10.00
World's Tiniest Porcelain Card (Limited Edition)	25.00
Michael Jordan with Tune Squad Gold Plate	35.00
CD with Cards (Nike)	35.00
Jumpman Poster with Cards	25.00
Marvin the Martian's Countdown Rock-o-Torn	15.00
Michael Jordan Cosmic Court	35.00
Moran Arishid	25.00
Space Jammin' Book	20.00
Space Jam Stand-Up from Theater	15.00
McDonalds Place Mats	1.00
Tune Squad Short Set	35.00
Michael Jordan Jacket	86.00
Michael Jordan Cologne	75.00

WHEATIES CEREAL BOXES

Boxes typically are collected in three forms: full and unopened, opened and resealed, and folded flat. Each is widely accepted and a matter of personal taste. The prices are based on Mint boxes in any of these forms. For easier identification, refer to series numbers, found at the bottom of the left side panel.

MISCELLANEOUS

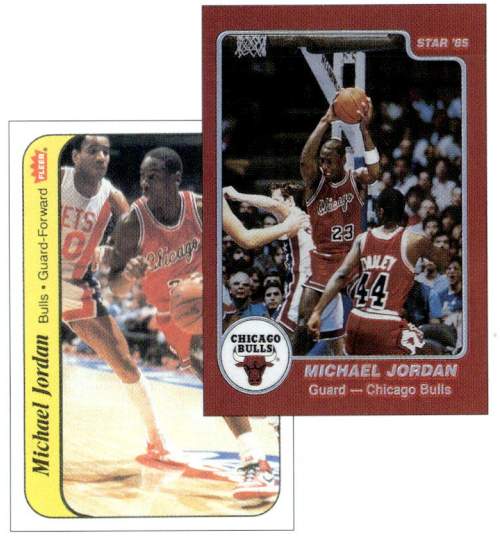
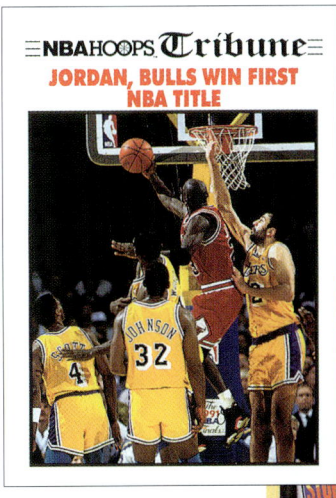

Year	Description	No.	Price
1988	First Edition	53	100.00
1988	Pouring ($5 Video Rebate)	14	50.00
1989	Eating Cereal (12/18 ounces)	70	45.00
1989	Eating Cereal (12/18 ounces)	73	45.00
1989	Eating Cereal (18 ounces)	78Z	30.00
1989	Champ. Tradition Continues	36	45.00
1989	Green Poster/Video Offer	73Z	50.00
1989	Blue Poster/Video Offer	73Z	50.00
1989	Purple Poster/Video Offer	73Z	50.00
1989	Story/Video Offer	56	25.00
1989	Story Part 2 (18 ounces)	57	40.00
1990	Pouring Cereal (12/18 ounces)	86Z	40.00
1990	Champ. Tradition Continues (12 ounces)	46	45.00
1990	Blue With Poster	64/43A	55.00
1990	Green With Poster	64/43B	55.00
1990	Purple With Poster	64/43C	55.00
1991	Eating Cereal (.75 ounce)	27	8.00
1991	Sweatsuit With Bag (12 ounces)	34	40.00
1991	Eating Cereal (18 ounces)	87	25.00
1991	Pouring Cereal (18 ounces)	86	20.00
1991	Air Jordan Calendar	82/82Z/83	30.00
1991	Shoot Hoops With Jordan	8	40.00
1991	Sweatsuit With Bag (18 ounces)	47K	20.00
1992	Super Single (1 Ounces)	1	8.00
1992	Super Single (1.5 Ounces)	2	8.00
1992	Air Jordan (18 ounces)	34	75.00
1992	Cards Isiah Thomas (18 ounces)	48E	18.00
1992	Cards Jordan (18 ounces)	48F	30.00
1992	Cards Bird/Rodman (18 ounces)	48G	25.00
1992	Cards Scottie Pippen (18 ounces)	48H	20.00
1992	Cards Charles Barkley (18 ounces)	49A	20.00
1992	Cards Karl Malone (18 ounces)	49B	20.00
1992	Cards Patrick Ewing (18 ounces)	49C	20.00
1992	Cards David Robinson (18 ounces)	49D	20.00
1993	Silver Commemorative (18 ounces)	91	18.00
1993	Silver Commemorative Canadian	91	35.00
1993	Playing Golf	75	35.00
1995	He's Back	18	18.00
1995	Video Game Offer	28	20.00
1996	Space Jam	71	8.00

SUPERCOLLECTOR

Say hello to the world's most devoted Michael Jordan collectors. Boy, do they have stories to tell!

The Jordanaires

There's a lavishly dressed man in Arkansas who's got 11 MJ Fleer Rookie Cards, and he's not even halfway through one of his objectives.

A teacher in Pennsylvania not only collects Jordan, she works him into her second-grade lesson plans, and then preaches his strengths to her varsity basketball team.

A chap in Alabama is so devoted to His Airness that he works two jobs — one to pay the bills, the other to buy his Bull.

A guy in Kentucky can't keep his Jordan collection confined to just one room . . . or two rooms . . . or even two rooms, two closets and a chest of drawers.

And then there's that well-mannered man in Maryland who's not that big into cards (he's only got around 800), and instead chases the items that really present a chase.

Indeed, when we called out for the ultimate Michael Jordan collectors in January, we expected brilliance. What we got, though, was, well, something truly befitting the greatest basketball player in the world.

More than 400 letters rolled in, each and every one worthy of applause and serious consideration. But since features on 400 Jordan collectors would require a magazine the size of a telephone book, we chose our top five.

Bulk was considered; variety was, too. We looked at diversity and origi-

By Tracy Hackler

nality, and we were interested in the stories of personal significance behind the passion. It made for tough decisions.

For everyone who wrote to us, we say, "Thanks." If you didn't make the cut, please don't take it personal; and by all means, don't stop collecting.

After all, if memory serves us correctly, there was a time when a certain teenager in North Carolina was cut from his high-school basketball team.

Anybody recall whatever happened to that guy?

CHARLES CATE
SPRINGDALE, ARK.

"I'm just glad he's not [No.] 45 still."

That's a harmless enough quote

MICHAEL JORDAN COLLECTIBLES 129

SUPERCOLLECTOR

Charles Cate, Springdale, Ark.

SUPERCOLLECTOR

until you consider the potential financial severity of the speaker's plight.

Mary Cate, Charles' wife, knew how big a hit the Cate family budget would've sustained had Jordan not gone back to his familiar No. 23.

Charles, you see, has an objective that won't go unrealized. He wants 23 1986-87 Fleer Jordan Rookies. To date he has 11.

"That's my goal; I'd like to have 23 of them to match his number," Charles says with the pride that only a man almost halfway through such a goal can muster. "I'd like to get 'em as quick as I can, before he quits playing, but that might be this year."

The most Cate's paid for a Fleer RC is $900, and that one's still in its pack with a stick of gum, a Jordan sticker and a Patrick Ewing RC to boot. The least he's paid is $200. Four of his 11 RCs could be considered Mint, and none, he says, "are junk."

Charles, 57, retired from Tyson Foods about five years ago to help his wife with her daycare business; he now sets up at shows on weekends.

"I collect a lot," Cate says. "And as I kept collecting, I ended up getting so many duplicates that I decided to start doing shows."

Don't worry, Cate doesn't sell any Jordan stuff unless he has dupes (the Fleer RCs being the obvious exception).

He's been harvesting Jordan for about five years, and when he started, he went "stark raving crazy."

How crazy?

"Oh goodness . . . man, oh man . . . oh, gosh," Cate utters, grasping to come up with the right words. "I own everything from cookie jars to drinking straws to party favors; games, golfing sets, all the McDonald's stuff, all the figurines, bed spreads, draperies, a sofa, popcorn still in the can, all the basketballs, all the big statues. It's unbelievable all the cards [I have], all the clothing, all the posters, walkie-talkies, backpacks, Jell-O, cups, bowls, coloring books . . . I've got it, bud. I've got a lot of stuff."

And get this: That's just the stuff in the Space Jam segment of Cate's Jordan collection.

Including his Jordan dupes, Cate estimates a card collection numbering better than 8,000, including 3,000 different cards.

But in an ensemble that includes several UDA autographed items, 11 Fleer Rookies and all the good Star stuff, Space Jam stands out.

"Truthfully, I like my Space Jam stuff," Cate insists. "That's the stuff that I'm proudest of, and the stuff that I wouldn't part with."

Cate, who says he's often mistaken for a member of the Bulls organization because of his lavish Bulls jewelry and team clothing, networks with hobbyists from Kentucky, New York, Chicago, Colorado, California and Florida to maintain his inventory.

He owns 20 pairs of Air Jordans, 15 watches, three signed UDA jerseys, a UDA bat, a UDA golf ball, and a healthy supply of autographed publications.

In May, Cate augmented his stash when he purchased a 900-card Jordan lot from a dealer in Rising Star, Texas, that included another 1985-86 Star Jordan and Cate's 11th Fleer RC.

If you're ever at a show and notice a fella decked out in full Bulls regalia, a guy sporting a thick gold chain holding a Bull's-head pendant with rubies for eyes and some 15 diamonds, there's a good chance that's Charles Cate, "The Jordan Man."

The Toyota 4-Runner outside with the Jordan license plates should also tip you off. And if it didn't, then the trailer it's towing with the other

SUPERCOLLECTOR

Lorne Grey Hall, Saylersville, Ky.

Jordan license plate certainly should've.

And if you've got a Jordan RC or two to sell . . . .

CHARLES CATE ON . . .

Why Jordan: "My son-in-law used to collect cards and that got me and my wife interested. So one day she just says, 'Let's collect Jordan cards.' That's just a player she liked because of his smile and his good attitude with kids and all.

"We just started going to card shops all the time, and it just kept growing."

What's next: "The [1997-98] autographed Upper Deck Game Jersey card. It books for $8,000. That's one of the most important ones."

When retirement's a reality: "I'll probably still keep looking for the cards that I don't own. But I'll probably quit collecting as heavy as I'm doing right now, and eventually, I'll give the collection to my grandson, Tyler Booth."

JILL STEFFEN HALIFAX, PA.

It started, like it so often does, with a six-pack. Usually, that's all it takes to get hooked.

Rarely, though, does it get to this point.

Jill Steffen of Halifax, Pa.

It begins way back in 1982, when Jill Steffen, the second-grade teacher and former collegiate two-guard, got her first taste . . . of Jordan mania, silly, via a six-pack of Carolina Blue soda honoring the Tar Heels' 1982 NCAA championship.

"That was my first piece of memorabilia, and it's probably still my favorite," Steffen says proudly. "I don't think I'd want to drink it, though."

The lesson to be learned here, of course, is simple: Don't drink — and strive.

Steffen calls her second-grade classroom an MJ shrine, full of student-made artwork, posters and promotional displays. Of the room's four walls, three are consumed with Jordan. And rarely does one of her lesson plans not include a Jordan hook.

"I teach the kids about Michael's work ethic and I teach them about role models," says the 30-year-old mother of three. "Michael has such a positive influence on so many people. He has so many things that young kids can take from him. I'd just like to say

SUPERCOLLECTOR

Nathan Carraway, Daphne, Ala.

thanks, for whatever it's worth."

Steffen, also the girls basketball coach at Millersburg (Pa.) Area High School, always wanted to be like Mike.

During her days as a shooting guard for Lycoming College in Williamsport, Pa., where she averaged almost 10 points a game, she kept a picture of Jordan in her locker, wore No. 23 on her socks and kept her dorm room stocked with All Things Jordan.

Today, she's got more than 1,300 cards and countless other collectibles. In fact, husband Kevin shelved his own interests to help Jill.

"He put his Don Mattingly collection on the sideburner so that he could help me focus on Jordan," she says. "[Collecting] is something that we enjoy doing together. With all of our attention focused on our children [Lindsay, 6, and 5-year-old twins Lauren and Elizabeth], collecting Jordan is something that the two of us really enjoy doing together."

Although Steffen's hesitant to pinpoint one card as her favorite ("I love them all," she says), she relents.

"If I had to pick one, I'd say the 1992-93 Fleer Team leader [#4]," she says. "It's not flashy or anything; there's just something about that card."

Steffen's stash is more than just 1,300 cards, though. Her most cherished items, in addition to the six-pack, is a brick from old Chicago Stadium that she received as a birthday gift from Kevin, and an authentic Jordan jersey "from a very dear friend."

She's got nine Bradford Exchange plates, two Hanes displays, six Wheaties boxes, puzzles, bobbing-head dolls, three autographs, an MJ organ donor card, a 1984 Sporting News, TV Guides and 24 *Becketts*.

More than any of that, though, she's teaching the next generation of Jordan hopefuls how to be like Mike.

And that collection is absolutely priceless.

JILL STEFFEN ON . . .

Why Jordan: "I started playing organized basketball when I was in third grade, and I wanted to find a player who I could connect with. I chose him because of the fact that he was cut from his high school team, and that didn't stop him. He wanted to be so much better.

"His work ethics are just to be modeled by everybody. As a coach, that would be my model work ethic for my team."

What's next: "My ultimate collectible, the thing I would love to own, is a pair of autographed sneakers or a basketball. I will have one of those items soon."

When retirement's a reality: "I will cry. I probably won't watch the NBA anymore. I love college basketball and the only reason I watch the NBA is because of Michael."

NATHAN CARRAWAY DAPHNE, ALA.

There are several ways, each with its own considerable validity, to measure your devotion to a player.

For 23-year-old Nathan Carraway, it's a second job, the proceeds from which go exclusively to funding his Jordan habit.

He installs security systems with his father during the week. That paycheck puts food on the table. On the weekend, he works in a card shop inside a Pro Image store at Springdale Mall in Mobile, Ala. For six years, that paycheck's put Jordans in his collection.

"That's my extra money that [my fiancee] can't touch," Carraway insists. "That's pretty much always been what's fed my Jordan addiction."

He's been gathering Jordan stuff in all shapes and sizes for the last 10 years and admits to spending roughly $300 a month to sustain his collection. But one

SUPERCOLLECTOR

Kevin Beck, Silver Spring, Md.

SUPERCOLLECTOR

card among his more than 6,000 stands out. And it's not the one you might imagine. Oh sure, he's got both high-dollar Jordan Rookies, but no one publishes a price guide that tracks sentimental value.

"I think my favorite piece is his second-year card [1987-88 Fleer #59], just because that particular card is the first card I ever bought of Jordan," Carraway says. "I liked Jordan, but when you're 13, you can't really swing much stuff, but I got my dad to get that Jordan. Sentimentally, that's my most valuable."

Carraway's parents also are responsible for one of Nathan's other favorites — the Jordan-signed jersey from UDA that he got for Christmas, the same jersey that had hung in Pro Image for about a year.

Carraway figures his Jordan collection — everything included — consists of about 7,000-8,000 items (hey, what's a thousand items between friends?). He owns 325 Jordan-graced magazines, including every *Beckett*, 16 Wheaties Boxes, 20 plates, and a piece of the floor and a brick from old Chicago Stadium.

He's kept a bevy of Jordan-based McDonald's memorabilia, and he's forced to store posters in dresser drawers because his walls have long been covered.

When it comes to cards, working in a card store has its advantages.

"The owner [Sid Ponder] has been super nice to me," Carraway says. "If somebody brings in a real high-dollar Jordan, he'll get it and we'll work something out. Mr. Ponder's helped a lot. If it wasn't for him, I wouldn't have a lot of the things that I do."

The same can be said for Nathan's fiancee, Kathleen, although she was initially reluctant to purchase Jordan items for her husband-to-be.

"Whenever a birthday or Christmas would roll around, she didn't want to buy me anything that I already had," he says. "That first year, we went through Christmas and she bought me some kind of on-line card-trader catalog or something that I never used. The next year she got me a Michael Jordan picture that I've got up on my wall. Now, if we go to any other card shop, she runs and gets me [and says], 'Do you have this one? Do you have this one?' She's helped me out a lot lately."

Sounds like a keeper to us, Nathan.

NATHAN CARRAWAY ON . . .

Why Jordan: "I was born in North Carolina, and when I was little, my mom always called me her 'little Tar Heel,' and I didn't really know what that was. So my mom and my dad sat me down and watched Tar Heel basketball games, and that was the time when Jordan was there. From then on, I was in awe of everything he was doing."

What's next: "One of those Game Jersey cards. I think I'll eventually get it, but I'm not gonna go rip open 100 cases of Upper Deck to get it."

When retirement's a reality: "From a collecting standpoint, I probably have a lot more money in my pocket now, or I'll be able to save up and afford one of those $2,000-$3,000 cards.

"You don't want it to end, but once it does it's over. I'm running out of room and it drains my pocketbook, but that's something that I've never minded the whole time I've been doing this. I suppose I'll miss it a lot, because I'll pretty much stop collecting."

LORNE GREY HALL
SAYLERSVILLE, KY.

Some extreme collectors devote a room to their stash. Others may donate a room and throw in some closet space for good measure.

Not Lorne Grey Hall, the 22-year-

SUPERCOLLECTOR

old Jordan junkie from Saylersville, Ky., whose got a vanity license plate that reads "Lorne 23," and a girlfriend who buys him Jordan underwear "all the time."

"I live in a trailer by myself and my whole trailer is decorated with [Jordan memorabilia]," Hall says. "I've got two bedrooms full and my living room's decorated with it."

Hall struggles to place a finite number of items in his collection, and ultimately opts to list the significant stuff.

• more than 950 cards

• more than 100 magazines ("All in Mint condition and stored in plastic cases," he notes.)

• several pieces of memorabilia from Chicago's 1991 NBA championship

• more than 30 shirts

• "tons" of life-size Gatorade stand-ups

• 35 posters

• "every Starting Lineup that's been made of Jordan"

• 10 pairs of Air Jordan shoes

• more than 200 Bulls games on tape ("My favorite is the time he scored the double nickel [55 points] against the Knicks when he came back [after retirement].")

Hall pegs his most prized collectible without much hesitation: MJ's 1986-87 Fleer RC, a Mint gem he picked up a year ago from his uncle for $500. As for the item packing the most sentimental value, well, that one's easy, too. It's an Air Jordan jacket from 1985 that Hall's outgrown only physically.

The notoriety of Hall's collection is such that he fields calls all the time from people wanting to buy stuff from him; he's yet to fill any orders.

"I've got about everything that I've ever seen, but I'm always looking," Hall says. "It's great to see so much stuff out on the market. I can see what I have and what I don't."

Hall's seen his idol play in person twice, both times during exhibition games in Kentucky.

"I saw him in 1991 and that was unreal, I mean unreal," says Hall, who's been collecting nothing but Jordan since 1989. "It was the most exciting thing I've ever seen. I also saw him play an exhibition game two years ago."

LORNE GREY HALL ON . . .

Why Jordan: "I'd have to say just the way he holds himself on the court, and his good sportsman attitude. And he's just a good role model."

What's next: "I'm still looking toward the big ['84-85 Star XRC] Jordan Rookie. I'm gonna get it, there's no doubt."

When retirement's a reality: "Well, I'm gonna keep collecting as far as I know. I'm heading this week to get a tattoo. I'm getting the Jumpman symbol put on my left arm. It's kind of a retirement thing. I figure it'll be pretty cool."

KEVIN BECK SILVER SPRING, MD.

You could say the story behind Kevin Beck's passion for Michael Jordan is a bona fide page-turner.

Something about more than 350 magazines would lend indisputable credence to such a claim.

Indeed, what Beck, 32, "lacks" in cards — he has close to 800 — he more than makes up for with enough Jordan-graced magazines to fill a library.

Of his prized periodicals, Beck's proudest of his label-less Sports Illustrateds. As of May 11, he'd compiled 43 weekly issues of SI with MJ's picture on the cover, one weekly issue with Mike's name on the cover, one oversized "Year in Sports," three NBA season previews and three Bulls championship editions.

"No. 1, I love magazines because of bigger pictures," says Beck, who's quick to note that he was married to wife Jenny on July 23, 1994, 10 years to the day after MJ's second SI cover appearance.

"I love magazines. The tone of my collection is just really unique, hard-to-find items."

Granted, SIs aren't too terribly tough to locate; but the other two prominent segments of Beck's collection typically present more of a challenge.

"The three biggest things I wanted to get every one of were his Wheaties boxes, every SI with him on the cover and every media guide," Beck insists. "Not only are these things bigger, but they come in so many different shapes and sizes. And they're actually what was issued at that time in his life."

In addition to 21 different full-size Wheaties boxes, Beck's got each media guide, schedule and yearbook since Jordan's been a Bull, a 1992 USA Olympic Team media guide and a Birmingham Barons media guide from MJ's baseball days. ("A media guide isn't a picture on a card, it's actually what they used at that time in his career.")

Oh, and then there's all of Beck's McDonald's stuff: three translites, three stand-up displays, eight different unused french fry holders, three cups, all eight unopened Fitness Fun toys from '91, a retirement pin from '94 and a school folder from '85.

Clearly, when it comes to chasing the greatest athlete on earth, Beck's in it for the thrill of the hunt.

He's derived much satisfaction from seeking the most cherished of his hidden gems, including:

• a 1985 McDonald's place mat with a full-color picture of you know who. "He's got hair and it says, 'Fuel for Air Jordan,' " Beck says. "It's probably one of the most unique things [I own]. It's gorgeous."

• the invitation that went out to herald the opening of Mike's restaurant, the first menu, the second menu and the first children's menu.

• the 1985 Guy Laroche wristwatch cardboard sign. "I've been told by a number of people that it never went out to stores," Beck says proudly.

• each University of North Carolina yearbook and each ACC handbook.

All of this brings us to the one item that was harder than anything else for Beck to find: a leather-bound tribute to UNC's national title in 1982.

"I just love researching different places, looking for unique stuff," Beck says in defense of his affinity for the aloof Jordan collectible. "It's definitely more rewarding [than collecting just cards] because, basically, I need to keep an eye out for Jordan memorabilia in different places, places you wouldn't expect."

SUPERCOLLECTOR

KEVIN BECK ON . . .

Why Jordan: "As a basketball player myself, I believe that if you want to excel at something you should learn from the best. As a collector, I am attracted to the variety and colorful nature of Jordan memorabilia."

What's next: "The 1984-85 [Chicago Bulls] season ticket holder pamphlet. It's a nice color one with Jordan in an Olympic uniform dunking. I've seen a picture of it. I've seen one advertised, but when I called, they had already sold it."

When retirement's a reality: "Because of endorsements and how much he is highlighted and so forth, I don't think anything will change about my collection. I certainly won't change my collection. I don't think I'll ever run out of things to collect on Jordan."

Tracy Hackler is an editor for Beckett Publications.

SUPERCOLLECTOR

GOING ONCE, GOING TWICE ... GONE

Tom Gadus planned to auction off his amazing 2,352-piece Michael Jordan collection

Ever since seeing Michael Jordan play a preseason game in 1984 during his rookie year, Tom Gadus has taken a special interest in His Airness. That interest grew so intense that Gadus eventually became a collector, amassing one of the largest Michael Jordan card collections known to exist.

Since that game in '84, Jordan obviously has turned into a legend — and Gadus' card collection has taken on legendary proportions.

The Chicago Bulls superstar isn't quite ready to give up the game, but Gadus, now married with a 5-year-old daughter with a future to consider, is ready to give up his incredible collection. In fact, his 2,275 Jordan cards comprised the bulk of what was billed as "The Ultimate Michael Jordan Collection" that was put up for auction in March. "I believe," Gadus says, "I have about 99 percent of every Jordan card ever made."

"It's almost like ending a madness and being able to get back to a normal life," says the soft-spoken 36-year-old, who lives in Dyer, Ind. "There's no way I'm going to leave the hobby, because I've enjoyed it. But right now, the cards are going to take a backseat to my wife and daughter."

Gadus' collection, whose sale was scheduled for March 27 in Oakbrook, Ill., by the Mastro and Steinbach Auctions firm, was built following one guideline:

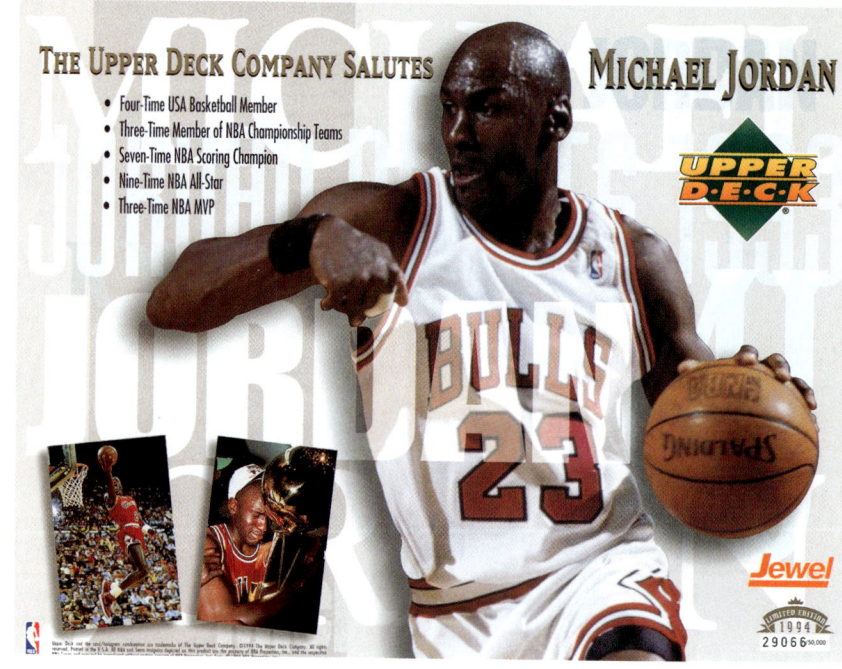

attempt to collect one of every card that features Jordan on it. This included all of Jordan's mainstream issues, regional and collegiate sets, foreign cards, baseball issues, oversize cards, promos, Broders and even cards showing Jordan in the background.

While Gadus casually collected Jordan's cards for fun during the 1980s, picking up various cards at shops or shows, it wasn't until the early 1990s — after the birth of his daughter, Brittany, and the Bulls' initial championship — that Gadus began collecting with a purpose and strategy.

"Initially, it was so easy," Gadus says. "And it was so inexpensive. It was fun. I loved Jordan and what he did for the city of Chicago. It was enjoyable. And at the time, I wasn't even thinking of the possibility of making any money off it. I was newly married and had no kids.

"But in the early '90s, when I started seeing [cards] that, in the mid-'80s, had cost me five, 10, 15 dollars and now five years later were worth a couple of hundred dollars, I started seeing the potential there," he adds.

SUPERCOLLECTOR

The potential, Gadus says, to one day create a nice little nest egg as insurance for this daughter's future. Based on the exploding value of the Jordan cards he already had in his possession and the assumption that any future Jordan cards had the potential to grow in value, Gadus decided to build a Jordan collection that would be second-to-none.

"When my daughter was born in 1991, I had bought a mutual fund in her name," he recalls. "But truthfully, I lost money with it the first couple of years, so I was looking for other investments. I looked up the cards I had and found out that I maybe had a $100 investment that, when you added the cards up at that time, might have been worth a couple of thousand dollars. So I said, 'Hey, this is a chance where I can make some money and also enjoy collecting Michael Jordan.'

"So I started collecting his cards and the companies started producing more and more and I saw the potential that, No. 1, I like Michael Jordan, and No. 2, I wanted to collect his cards because I enjoyed them," Gadus adds. "But truthfully, the most important thing was I saw the investment potential of them. I figured, assuming Michael and the Bulls continued to win championships and his image continued to be above reproach, that this would be the perfect opportunity for me to do something that I enjoyed, but also where I could, in future years, sell the collection and make some money and use the money toward my daughter's college education."

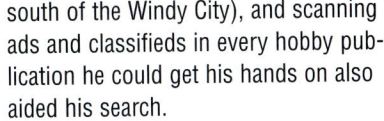

Initially, Gadus planned to collect Jordan's cards until the Bulls' star retired and then sell his collection when his daughter turned 18. But in the past year, Gadus has watched the hobby become inundated with more and more brands, inserts and subsets, a flooding of the market that opened Gadus' eyes.

"I figured now might be the time, where selling it in an auction might be the best opportunity for me," Gadus says.

In all, Gadus' collection totals 2,352 Jordan-related items, including all of Jordan's Kenner Starting Lineup figures, more than a dozen Wheaties cereal boxes and every precious metal Jordan medallion produced by The Highland Mint and Enviromint. Bill Mastro, who was to handle the auction, estimates the value to be at least $100,000.

"No value has been put on the endless amount of hours involved in assembling this collection," Mastro says. "The thousands of miles of travel, the thousands of letters and the hundreds of hours on the phone should be considered in the value of this collection. It could not be duplicated."

Gadus built his collection with plenty of help and leads from other Jordan collectors.

Regular visits to card shops and shows around the Chicago area (Dyer is located just south of the Windy City), and scanning ads and classifieds in every hobby publication he could get his hands on also aided his search.

"I'm not a fool to believe I've got every [Jordan card] ever made, but I think I'm pretty close," says Gadus.

He credits Chicago-based collector Oscar Gracia with helping him locate many of the tougher Jordan cards he owns. Once his Jordan collection is sold, Gadus plans to remain involved in collecting — albeit on a much smaller scale than before. He'll continue to collect Jordan cards and also plans to pursue some older baseball issues. If the opportunity arises, Gadus wouldn't mind buying Jordan cards on behalf of the buyer of his collection.

"Assuming the cards are sold and that I got at least a fair price, I would be willing to continue to purchase [Jordan] cards for the person who purchases the collection," Gadus says. "My thinking is the person . . . may be somebody who has the money, but they just don't have the time to go out and look for all the stuff. If I get a fair price, I could continue collecting all of Jordan's cards until he retires."

So while the collection soon will be gone, the desire still remains — the kind of desire even someone such as Jordan himself can appreciate.

Randy Cummings is a former editor of **Beckett Basketball Card Monthly.**

MICHAEL JORDAN COLLECTIBLES **141**

SUPERCOLLECTOR

JORDAN JUNIORS
YOU DIDN'T THINK OUR TRIBUTE TO THE WORLD'S GREATEST JORDAN EXTREMISTS WAS LIMITED TO ADULTS, DID YOU?

Isaac Chavez, 12.

Jared Callahan
Age: 15
Hometown: Lodi, Calif.

Why Mike: "My mom and I went into the neighborhood sports card shop, and she asked [the dealer] who would be a good guy for my son to collect. He said, 'Michael Jordan.' We went home, and there happened to be a Bulls game on TV. I just loved his moves, and all the flying around. It was magical."

Cards: 668

Favorite card: "I have two favorite cards: The 1992-93 Upper Deck 15,000 Point Club [#PC4], and then the 1992-93 Stadium Club Beam Team [#1]. I bought the Beam Team for $6. It went up to $100; that's when I realized the value of Michael Jordan."

Favorite non-card collectible: "That would be my plaque that's signed by Michael Jordan — that's the only real signature I have of his. My mom gave me that one, too. I don't let anybody touch it."

Collecting dream: "I admire him as a person and everything, but I'd love to just shoot around with him, and have him see what I've done [with his collectibles]. Just to say, 'This is what I do.'"

When I'm older . . . "It'll go one of two ways. It'll completely diminish and I'll become bored with it, or I'll have a higher paying job other than a paper boy and I'll have all these elaborate pieces. I think it'll probably go toward the latter."

Isaac Chavez
Age: 12
Hometown: Grand Island, Neb.

Why Mike: "It's something to do. It's a hobby so I don't get, like, bored. And I watch almost all the [Bulls'] games."

Cards: 700

Favorite card: "My $1,000 one. The [1986-97] Fleer Rookie. It's old, it's original and it's collectible, too. I've had it for 11 years. I didn't pull it; my brother [Raymond] gave it to me."

Favorite non-card collectible: "My Jordan stand-up. It's [showing] that one free-throw dunk he does. He's, like, up in the air."

Collecting dream: "To get a thousand cards, and to meet him in person, too. That's one of the things I really want."

When I'm older . . . "I'll probably still collect Jordan. I'll collect him 'til he retires, or until I can't find any more."

Jared Callahan, 15.

SUPERCOLLECTOR

Frankie Gonzalez, 15.

Frankie Gonzalez
Age: 15
Hometown: Carolina, Puerto Rico

Why Mike: "Initially, his play, you know. I saw him play once and it was amazing."

Cards: 1,566

Favorite Card: "My favorite card is the Fleer Rookie. I've had it for about two years; I bought it at a card store around here."

Favorite non-card collectible: "My four Starting Lineup figures. I don't have a favorite, I like them all."

Collecting dream: "To meet him and show him my cards. Maybe it'll happen. Anything's possible."

When I'm older . . . "I've been collecting Jordan for six years, so I guess I'll just keep collecting. I'll stop when I have all of his cards."

Dylan Benton
Age: 13
Hometown: Raleigh, N.C.

Why Mike: "He's the best. He's just better than everyone else, and I just think he's a great role model. Plus, he went to school at UNC, which is where I hope to go."

Cards: 650

Favorite Card: "The Gold Refractor from 1997-98 Finest. It's numbered 289 out of 289 — the last one in the set. We traded for that one. I've never pulled anything that big."

Favorite non-card collectible: "An autographed hat band that came from his golf tournament."

Collecting dream: "The [1984-85 Star] Jordan Rookie. I've never actually seen one in person. I've heard of a few guys selling it, but I've never been able to get it."

Dylan Benton, 13.

When I'm older . . . "I'm just going to continue going to collector shops like I do with my dad right now, and check out the newspapers for Jordan items. And I'll keep looking for anything I don't have."

MICHAEL JORDAN COLLECTIBLES **143**

Market Analysis

Michael Jordan a card collector? Perhaps. Recently, he speculated that his wife had accumulated at least three of every one of his cards. He went on to add that there were boxes and boxes of his cards lying around his house, ostensibly to be passed along to his kids and grandkids.

No doubt, Jordan also has plenty of Air Jordan sneakers, old jerseys and other keepsakes from his amazing career that he's hoarding away for future enjoyment. If so, one could surmise that the Bulls legend anticipates a bull market for his cards and other memorabilia at some point in the future.

In truth, he need not worry. Jordan's cards and collectibles are outrageously popular today and will probably only increase in value — both in terms of what they'll mean to those who own them and with regard to the price tag they'll command — once he has retired for good and soars to new heights in the business world.

Jordan's popularity knows no boundaries with collectors. Men, women and children all love him, and it really doesn't matter if they're a Chicago Bulls fan or not. They stand in awe of his once-in-a-lifetime skills as a player, are captivated with his looks,

By Randy Cummings

dress and style and rush to own anything linked to him.

"He's the Babe Ruth of our era," notes Tim Jostes, a Chicago-area sports memorabilia dealer. "Michael Jordan will always be collectible."

The market for his collectibles continues to be the strongest among any of today's active athletes because adults recognize his presence as one of sports' all-time great icons. And youths idolize him, in part for his highlight-reel talents as a basketball player, but also because he's the most skillfully-marketed athlete in history.

Everybody may not want to "be like Mike," they just want a piece of Mike.

"Of kids who are 13 years old today, how many are going to want one of his jerseys or balls or an autograph when they're 30?" Jostes says. "As kids, they can't afford a Michael Jordan jersey. But when they're 30, they probably can and will want to buy one.

"So, I just don't foresee [the values of] any of his stuff ever coming down."

Just like cards and other memorabilia linked to the late Mickey Mantle continue to enjoy success in today's market, so too will Jordan's collectibles be cherished for generations to come. Mantle's items were purchased largely by adults as reminders of their child-

Market Analysis

hood and the man they idolized. So, too, will be Jordan's.

Consider, though, that this is an age in which sports memorabilia is an industry, which means more companies are producing more products than ever imaginable in Mantle's playing days. Whereas Mantle appeared on fewer than 200 trading cards while in pinstripes, Jordan appears on nearly that many every couple of seasons. Yet, it appears with Jordan collectibles that there's never been a saturation point,

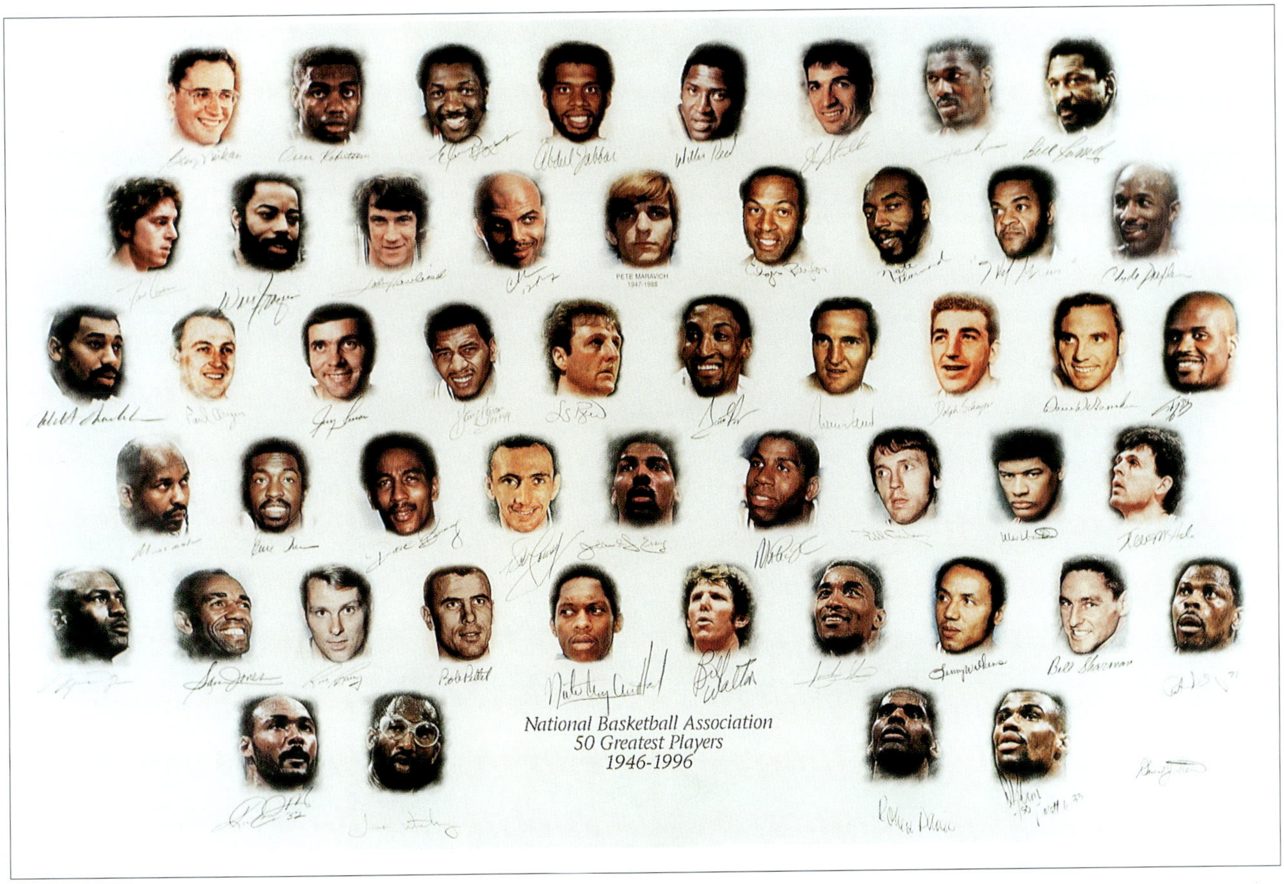

MICHAEL JORDAN COLLECTIBLES 147

Market Analysis

where the sports collecting marketplace has witnessed too many collectibles for too few collectors. If anything, there are so many collecting-conscious sports fans who admire Jordan that there will always be a market for His Airness.

"It's all relative," Jostes says. "Your audience is so much greater for Michael Jordan than anyone else."

Like his legend, Jordan's memorabilia should enjoy a healthy market for years to come.

Randy Cummings is a former editor of **Beckett Basketball Card Monthly.**

Photo Contributors

Andrew D. Bernstein / NBA Photos

Andy Hayt / NBA Photos

AP / World Wide Photos

Bill Smith

Bill Smith / Sports Illustrated

Brian Spurlock

Nathaniel S. Butler / NBA Photos

Courtesy of Nike

Patrick Murphey-Racey / Sports Illustrated

Reuters / Corbis-Bettmann

Rocky Widner

Courtesy of Upper Deck Authenticated

Walter Iooss Jr. / Sports Illustrated